DOWN

IS NOT

OUT

Teenagers and Depression

DOWN
IS NOT
OUT

Teenagers and Depression

ESSIE E. LEE and RICHARD WORTMAN, M.D.

JULIAN MESSNER
NEW YORK

Published by Julian Messner,
A Division of Simon & Schuster, Inc.
Simon & Schuster Building
Rockefeller Center
1230 Avenue of the Americas
New York, New York 10020

10 9 8 7 6 5 4

JULIAN MESSNER and colophon are
trademarks of Simon & Schuster, Inc.

Manufactured in the United States of America

Library of Congress Cataloging-in-Publication Data

Lee, Essie E.
  Down is not out.

  Bibliography: p.
  Includes index.
  Summary: Discusses mental depression, its causes,
its effects, and some of the ways it can be dealt
with.
  1. Depression in children—Juvenile literature.
2. Youth—Mental health—Juvenile literature.
[1. Depression, Mental. 2. Youth—Mental health.
3. Mental health] I. Wortman, Richard, 1943–
II. Title.
RJ506.D4L44   1986   616.85'27   85-26031
ISBN 0-671-52613-8

CONTENTS

One—Who Are You?

Are you the lonely
one that I heard about
The one that can't find
some form of salvation?
I know you; I know
what you stand for one.
I know what you mean;
the lonely soul without a
friend. I can imagine
you in the daytime with the gloomy sun.
Sitting, standing, not knowing
what to do. At night you
try to fix up your mind
with the stars looking at you.
You're so confused and so
lonely. Why one? Why are
you this way? Why are you
so mysterious and full of
anxiety and sadness? You see
in a world of nobody and nowhere
Nobody understands you one. Nobody
except maybe me!*

---
*From *Burning Dreams: Poems by Young Adults,* Greicy Rubiera,
ed., New York State Poet in The Schools and the St. Luke's
Adolescent After-School Program, New York, 1984.

INTRODUCTION

"What is it like being a teenager?" This question was asked of a group of adolescents waiting on line in front of Madison Square Garden in New York City early in July 1985. They spent many hours lounging in the uncomfortable humid weather, hoping to be lucky enough to get a ticket for the Madonna concert.

ANN: It's okay.

BOB: Lots of hassles—Do's and Don'ts.

PHIL: Best time of your life—carefree.

CURTIS: A waiting period—too young or too old.

PAM: Yeah. Wait until you're grown up.

TED: For me a lot of pressures. No job!

DEBBIE: Lots of decisions.

BAIRD: What am I going to be? If there is a world left!

DONNA: I'm almost eighteen. I'll be free soon. But I don't want to be.

TIFFANY: Very, very scary.

RICK: Between the environment and nuclear warheads, we're an endangered species.

Adolescence is said to be a most stressful stage in one's development. Yet the majority of youths adapt to rapidly changing events without too much trouble. They learn to cope with the physiological revolution of their own bodies' maturation, find comfort in their own sub-cultures, appear to take pride in their appearance and its effect on peers, aspire to school achievement, and explore career choices.

Adolescents are constantly becoming—either someone they don't like or someone they do like. To improve their relationships with peers, parents, and other adults, young people work on becoming aware. They learn to understand other people and themselves as they assume control and responsibility for their actions and their lives.

Living spontaneously is normal for this age group. But so are the pressures from peers, parents, school, and the social environment. These stresses often lead to temporary periods of mild anxiety and depression. However, for some young people, depression can be a serious illness that limits functioning, effectiveness, and growth. This book examines some of the pressures within the adolescents' world, their coping skills, and the network of interacting people who provide support.

DOWN

IS NOT

OUT

Teenagers and Depression

CHAPTER 1

Depression: What It Is, What It Isn't, and What It May Be

Most teenagers feel sad and discouraged at times. Some feel so unhappy that they are always ready to cry, even when parents or teachers just raise their voices or when friends kid them a little. Sometimes they may not even know why they are crying. Teenagers may sometimes feel so bad that everything seems hopeless and life doesn't seem worth living. These sad feelings can be called a depression. Some psychiatrists, psychologists, social workers, and nurses say that such a person is "having a depression." They are describing more than just sad feelings. People who are in a depression show other symptoms, such as difficulty sleeping, boredom, lack of energy, difficulty concentrating on schoolwork, irritability, and bad feelings about themselves. All of these things together make up a clinical depression, which is a mental disorder. You may feel sad or depressed and not have a depression, but if you have a depression, you do feel sad and you also have other symptoms.

1

Normal Moodiness

Everyone, young and old, feels sad sometimes, but these feelings may come more often to a teenager than to an older person. That is why young people are sometimes said to be moody. This does not mean that they are sad most of the time, but just that they have sad feelings frequently. These feelings may bother the teenager more than an older person who has gotten used to normal ups and downs. What happened to Susan is a good example of how small things may bother a teenager and cause sadness for a short time.

Susan, who is fourteen, returned home from school crying one day. Her mother was surprised, because Susan was usually a happy person. It seems that Susan waited for her friends at an appointed meeting place for an hour, but they failed to show up. She had already felt down, because she had not done very well on an English paper. She had looked forward to sharing her disappointment with her friends and checking out how well they had done. Because she was already feeling upset, her friends' failure to show up was unusually painful for Susan. She began to wonder if her friends really liked her. Her mother listened to her story and tried to make Susan feel better. Susan was able to stop crying, but she had trouble falling asleep that night.

Susan awoke the next morning feeling better, but she still wondered why her friends had stood her up. Feeling a little uncomfortable, Susan asked one of them what had happened. When she learned that she had been waiting in the wrong place for her friends and that they were sorry about what happened, Susan felt a lot better. Her sadness was a normal reaction to the sort of disappointment every young person endures from time to time.

Reactive Depression

Every teenager faces many minor traumas. At the time they occur, they seem major and cause serious unhappiness. Usually, in a couple of days, both the disappointment and the sad feelings are forgotten. Sometimes, however, these feelings do not go away so quickly, and the teenager may suffer other uncomfortable feelings, thoughts, and behavior. One teenager may feel bored and not enjoy anything. Another may become irritable and get angry with parents, teachers, and friends for no apparent reason. If feelings of anger and resentment toward parents, brothers, and sisters become too great—as they did with Judd, whom you will read about later—this may lead the adolescent to run away from home. A third teenager may feel very lonely and think that no one wants to be his or her friend. Other young people may not be able to concentrate on their schoolwork. This can lead to slipping grades and possible failure. For others, the unhappiness can lead to physical aches and pains, loss of appetite, and tiredness. Any of these difficulties can make young people feel that something is wrong with them. After a while they may begin to believe that, and then they feel that they really don't deserve to be happy.

A young person who continues to have these feelings for more than two weeks is not just going through normal adolescent moodiness, however. A good example of extended mild depression occurred when David broke his arm. He was just starting his junior year of high school, and before the first football game of the season, he broke his arm during practice. He had not played much the previous year, but he thought he had a good chance this season. When he broke his arm, however, all of his hopes were shattered. He knew he would be out for the entire season.

The rest of David's life was fine. He had good friends and was a capable student. His parents respected him and gave him as much freedom as he wanted. They were proud of his football-playing, but cared about him just as much whether he played football or not. The coach asked David to come to practice so that he could at least learn the plays for the following year. He was invited to sit on the bench with the rest of the team during the games. His parents, friends, and coach went out of their way to convince David that they still respected him and wanted him to be a part of the team. But David felt that he had let both himself and the others down by breaking his arm, and being around his teammates just made him feel worse. Not only did he stay away from his teammates, but he avoided his other friends, too. David had a feeling that they might not want to be seen with him, since he was no longer a football player. His grades went down that semester, because he had trouble concentrating on homework, and he didn't seem to care very much about anything. Not until the last game of the season did he feel like sitting with the team. After that, David again enjoyed being with his friends and began to study hard. His grades went up the next semester.

David experienced a real disappointment and was understandably upset. But his loss of self-esteem, his avoidance of friends, and his inability to study were not just normal adolescent moodiness. He fell into a mild depression and did not become his normal self again for several months, despite the extra support from his family and friends. For some reason, David was unable to adapt to his loss as quickly as would have been expected. He felt bad about himself for some time, in spite of the encouragement everybody gave him. This shows that his ability to adapt was not well developed. He certainly did not have a severe emotional disorder, but during those three months, David was quite unhappy. Another disappointment in the future might set off the same kind of depression.

Chronic Mild Depression

Some teenagers are depressed much of the time because something always seems to be going wrong. When several things go wrong, it becomes more and more difficult to bring everything back to normal. Then the teenager slowly loses self-confidence and begins to think that things are never going to work out. After a while, this young person comes to believe there is something wrong with the world and with him or her. This loss of hope and self-esteem is a serious thing.

Sandra suffered this kind of chronic unhappiness. She had trouble remembering a time when she really felt good. She thought things were better before her father left the family, when she was seven. She thought she was her father's favorite child. Sandra knew that her mother had always been closer to her older sister, who was seventeen, two years older than Sandra. Her mother always spoke badly of her father, blaming him for their financial problems, saying he was irresponsible. Sandra stuck up for her father even though she thought her mother was probably right.

For a while after he left, her father would telephone Sandra and promise to take her to the movies or shopping. She waited for him many times, but he did not come; and he forgot her birthday. Sandra began to wonder if she was worthwhile. Her mother scolded her and compared her to her father when Sandra forgot to make her bed or pick up her clothes. This made Sandra feel even more worthless.

Sandra stayed away from home as much as possible because she was so unhappy there. She spent a lot of time with her friends, looking to them to make her feel better. They liked her, but sometimes Sandra's need for attention bothered them and they teased her or avoided her. At times, Sandra thought that no one really liked her. It wasn't hard for her to believe this, since she didn't like herself very much. Thinking about what was wrong and trying to figure out how to get people to like her caused Sandra to have trouble falling asleep. These thoughts also made it hard for her to concentrate on her homework.

Sandra received a cocker spaniel puppy for Christmas from her uncle. The gift made her very happy, but after about a week, things started to go wrong again. Her mother began to criticize Sandra for not cleaning up after the dog. This took away some of the happiness of having a pet. She still enjoyed this cuddly animal who loved her and did not criticize her. Sandra never looked terribly sad, and she did okay at school and with friends, but she was never happy for long and did not do as well as she could have. Sandra had a chronic low-level depression, which she could not leave behind.

Major Depression

Although both David and Sandra were depressed, neither of them reached the depths of despair that can occur in a severe depression. They both continued to get along, although they were handicapped by their sadness and lack of confidence. When a depression becomes really severe, it is called a major depression and has many disabling symptoms. Dr. Subhash Inamdar, the unit chief of Adolescent Inpatient Services at Bellevue Psychiatric Hospital in New York City, found that most of the seriously depressed adolescents he saw had the following problems: loss of interest in almost all things, feelings of loneliness and of being unloved, boredom, loss of pleasure, suicidal thoughts, suicidal acts, poor concentration, feelings of worthlessness, social withdrawal, diminished school performance, running away, difficulty sleeping, and tiredness upon awakening. Dr. Richard Hudgens of Washington University Medical Center in St. Louis, Missouri, found additional symptoms in seriously depressed teenagers: loss of appetite and weight, trouble with memory, nervousness, decreased ability to do tasks, and feelings of hopelessness and guilt. This list of problems shows why a serious depression causes so much suffering.

These problems experienced by depressed teenagers are not much different from those felt by depressed adults. One difference between adults and teenagers, however, is that the depressed teenagers are more likely to think about suicide and even attempt to commit suicide. This makes depression in young people very serious indeed.

It is also striking how many areas of a teenager's life are affected by a major depression. Sexual activity may be one of them. Adolescents may confuse sexual attraction and passion for love when it is only infatuation. Often young people are not able to determine the difference between these two strong emotions. Rachel Swarns, seventeen, is a reporter for *New Youth Connection,* a monthly newspaper written by and for teenagers. She says, "Most teens are not emotionally ready for sexual relationships. At a time when teens should be developing lasting friendships and interests, we are burdening ourselves with unnecessary adult pressures. Worry over unwanted pregnancies and sexually transmitted diseases are things which we as teens should not have to deal with, especially since many of us are unprepared to deal with them."

Look at what happened to Mimi. She considered herself to be a social outcast. She was failing in school and fighting with her parents. Mimi had been called a fat pig by schoolmates since the third grade. At sixteen, she weighed more than 160 pounds. Because Mimi's crash dieting enabled her to lose ten to twenty pounds periodically, her clothes never fit her ever-changing figure. Makeup aggravated Mimi's pimples. Poor nutrition contributed to dull, lifeless, mousy brown hair. Mimi would do anything to have a boyfriend—and she did. She became a willing partner for one of the most handsome boys in the senior class. Their sexual activities became the talk of Johnson High. Mimi was eager to prove her love even though she knew the young man didn't share her feelings. When she became pregnant, Mimi's depression increased to the point of potential suicide. She wanted her baby as proof of an intimate relationship—although a one-sided and short-lived one—but the young man said he was not the baby's father. Like a character in a bad melodrama, Mimi was rejected by the only person she'd shared her feelings with and had physically loved.

Another example demonstrates how an adolescent can be affected by a major depression. Seventeen-year-old Jessica was a very moral and proper girl. She had sex for the first time with a boy she cared about very much. Unfortunately, she got gonorrhea, a serious venereal infection, from him. She received the necessary medical treatment, but her mother found out about the infection. Jessica claimed that she got it from a toilet seat. Her mother did not challenge this lie, but Jessica doubted that she really believed her. Jessica's doctor asked her to tell the boy about the infection so that he could be treated, too, but she was too embarrassed, angry, and hurt to do this. She broke off with the boy without an explanation.

After about two weeks, Jessica's intense feelings of anger and shame lessened, but she slowly began to feel sick. She was tired much of the time and developed pains in her stomach and constipation. She returned to her doctor for an examination. He told her that the infection was completely cured, and that he could find no reason for her new problems. He gave her a laxative for her constipation. A month later, she again returned to the doctor. Jessica now believed that her constipation

9

was causing a bad odor that others could smell. The doctor said there was no odor and no reason why she would have one, but instead of feeling better, Jessica was upset that he did not believe her.

She began to avoid her friends, because of the arguments she would get into with them. When they kidded her about anything, Jessica took it personally and became upset. She thought that her mother had become demanding and critical, and Jessica began to avoid her, too. She found herself increasingly alone. Although this was her choice, she felt lonely and unwanted and cried almost every day. Because of her unhappiness, she said to herself, "Why can't I be like everyone else?" Jessica thought of taking pills.

In school, where she had been a good student, Jessica was unable to pay attention. She no longer raised her hand in class, even when she forced herself to pay attention and knew the answer. When someone else answered the question, Jessica put herself down. She felt stupid.

Jessica lost her appetite, and over a period of six months she lost fifteen pounds. She also had trouble sleeping. In the morning, she felt very tired. Sometimes Jessica was late for her first class and would get into trouble with the teacher. Jessica remained worn out all day. She described her days as a "struggle against myself." But she continued to go to school and forced herself to study. She ate, even though she wasn't hungry. Jessica came to believe that life was a losing battle, and she began to feel more and more hopeless.

A major depression can affect every aspect of a teenager's life, as the story of Jessica shows. Jessica experienced almost all of the difficulties mentioned earlier. A real-life stress set off her depression. Yet after a partial recovery from the trauma of her venereal disease, Jessica's difficulties gradually got worse and worse, and more and more areas of her life were affected. She began to feel so bad that she believed awful things about herself—that she had a bad odor, for example. This distortion of reality can be present in the more severe cases of teenage depression, and it is very painful and dangerous. One sixteen-year-old boy heard voices in his head calling him "stupid" and "good for nothing." Sometimes these voices, or auditory hallucinations, actually tell depressed people to kill themselves.

Another part of Jessica's story is typical of adolescent depression. She described her mother in negative terms and said their relationship was terrible. In fact, her mother was not harsh and critical of Jessica. Although they did have minor disagreements, Jessica saw them as major battles. When Jessica began to feel better, she was surprised to find that her mother was not as hard on her as she thought during her depression. The two of them were able to get along together quite well.

When a person is in a depression, minor problems and difficulties seem worse than they really are, and past difficulties are also exaggerated. While growing up, Mimi had periods when she was really slim and presentable. But while she was depressed, she erased them from her mind. This kind of thinking makes the past seem worse than it was and the present seem worse than it is. It is like looking at the world through dark glasses. When looking to the future for possible relief, the person cannot remove those dark glasses, and so the future

11

looks just as bleak as the present. Consequently, a sense of complete hopelessness follows. This is the way Judd saw himself and his future.

When Judd was five years old, his grandfather was killed in a mine explosion, along with fifty-nine other men. Judd remembered the funeral: "It was eerie—no caskets, no bodies." The light of sixty candles flickering in the darkness of the church and the sobbing of men and women haunted him for years. His grandmother held Judd's hand and told the young boy to always remember that part of him was burned in the mine. Each night, as he prayed for his grandfather's soul, Judd tried to imagine what it would be like to be sealed in the darkness of that coal mine.

Four years later, when Judd was in school, he wrote short stories. The first ones were about the mine. But his later stories were about characters and places Judd saw on television. His heroes were spectacular figures—daring bank robbers, astronauts, mountain climbers, and sky pirates. Judd's love of science fiction led to an interest in engineering. But he was afraid to tell his family about it.

Then another cave-in took the life of Judd's oldest brother. Judd was thirteen and in the eighth grade. At the funeral, Judd's grandmother again reminded him of his relationship to the mine. Judd tried to tell her of his fear of being buried there and his desire to become an engineer. "You'll follow the life of all the Preston men," she told him sharply. The others—his parents, brothers, and sister—just laughed at Judd's ambitious plans. His fears were greatest at night, and often Judd didn't turn the light out in his bedroom until daybreak. After several months, he became so fearful and anxious that he couldn't eat or sleep. He stopped going to the library. There were times when Judd considered suicide as the only way of avoiding death in the mine. In the end, he decided to run away. Judd packed a knapsack with his favorite paperbacks, a harmonica, some T-shirts and jeans, a pocket knife, a few apples, and some cookies. Early one morning in August, Judd took $50 from his mother's cash box, hugged his dog, and quietly left the cement-block house. He would not die in the mine; he would become an engineer.

Hopelessness is a symptom of almost 90 percent of seriously depressed teenagers, and this makes it hard for the victims to get help. Hopelessness also can make suicide look like an attractive choice to the depressed teenager.

Living with an alcoholic parent can cause a sensitive child to become depressed. Because of the many responsibilities assumed by the youngster, school and friends get little attention. The child feels alienated and confused. In this depressive state, he cannot determine what is real and what is fantasy. But when the depressive state has passed, the young person can learn to divorce the alcohol from the true parent. Meanwhile, depression symptoms prevent the teenager from performing satisfactorily.

The director of the Rainbow Project in New York, a treatment program for children of alcoholic parents, reported the startling results of a questionnaire given to children in his program. "We were amazed at the number of young children aged seven to twelve who reported having tremors, going into the school supply closet and shaking for no apparent reason, having chronic stomachaches, having migraine headaches and

13

not reporting them to anyone. 'It's useless to report it at home,' they said, 'and you don't tell the teacher, because you're scared.' "

Sheldon has an alcoholic mother. The oldest of four children, Sheldon feels inadequate and guilty. No matter what he does, he cannot make things right at home. His peers admire his achievements both in and out of school, but Sheldon gets little satisfaction from their approval. He sets high standards for himself and is often supercritical of others. Now sixteen, Sheldon has grown used to the inconsistencies. One day his mother is warm and loving; the next, she's belligerent and hostile. Rules about curfew, bedtime hour, and visiting friends change without warning. And he has to adapt his own behavior to what is expected by the good mother or the bad mother.

As their minds develop, teenagers learn to look into the future. This can be a great help when making decisions about which courses to take in high school. But depressed teenagers see a future filled with more sadness and failure. This makes the present seem even more painful. In reality, the depression will probably improve and the future may be bright, even though everything seems terrible and hopeless at the moment.

Manic Depression

Nothing is further from depression than mania. When a person is manic, feelings of elation and power take over. It may seem that mania has no connection with depression and should not be discussed in this book, but depression and mania are closely bound together. In both conditions, a person's mood reaches an extreme; then it begins to control the person's thoughts and behavior. Some teenagers may have both disorders, first one and then the other. This condition is called a manic-depressive disorder. The person may be in the depths of depression in June and then be out of control with feelings of elation and power in August. This condition often first appears in adolescence and may begin as either mania or depression, although mania usually appears first.

This happened to Anna when she was sixteen and a junior in high school. She had always been a sweet, somewhat shy girl. A good student, she was in a special program to prepare for a health care career. Her family had always been very protective of their youngest daughter, who was their delight. The first signs of the disorder were not seen as problems and, in fact, were welcomed by teachers and friends. Anna became more and more assertive in her classroom participation and more outgoing in her interaction with friends. At home, she showed the beginning of defiance toward both her parents and a new teasing playfulness with her father. At first everyone saw this as normal adolescent development; it seemed like a good thing in a girl who had been rather shy and unassertive. Anna also revealed flashes of anger, unusual for her, but they did not last long. Because the family had always taken religion quite seriously, they were pleased with Anna's new enthusiasm for the church service where she sang and prayed loudly. She began to have some trouble falling asleep at night, but she was not tired during the day; she did not seem to need as much sleep as she had before.

At night, as Anna lay in bed, unable to fall asleep, she would think about her special relationship with God. At times, she believed that he had chosen her for some special purpose. Such ideas were acceptable as a part of her family's religious beliefs. Even the idea that she might be an angel did not seem impossible, since she had always been such a good person. The power that she was feeling made her a little uneasy, as did the increasing speed of the thoughts that came into her head. There were so many that she jumped from one to another, and so many things to do that she started many projects. But Anna never reached a decision and never completed anything she started. She had little control over her thinking or actions.

Anna's teachers became concerned when they noticed that her written compositions did not make any sense; she jumped from one idea to another. Her comments in class became more and more frequent and had little connection with what was being discussed. Also, Anna's increasing use of foul language seemed strange, because she was so religious. Even friends who used this language themselves felt uncomfortable and concerned when they heard Anna talk this way.

At home, she challenged her parents more and more often. When Anna did not get her way, she became intensely angry and swore at them. At times she appeared quite distressed, but this feeling was quickly replaced by elation. Finally, Anna was hardly sleeping at all. She talked rapidly, and although each statement made sense by itself, it had almost no connection with what preceded or followed it. Anna had very little insight into what was happening to her, and she didn't realize that she needed help. The manic experience itself was so

16

powerful that she could not step out of it for even a moment to question what was happening to her. In the end, her parents saw that her behavior was not normal, and they took Anna to a professional for help. The psychiatrist said that Anna was suffering from a severe manic mental disorder.

Anna's story is typical of the appearance of a manic disorder in adolescence. When it began, she appeared to be completely normal. Then, as things got worse, Anna began to seem like a different person. But finally, although many things about her kept changing, her elated mood and increased energy appeared central to all of the other changes in thinking and behavior.

Three months after Anna recovered and returned to normal, she had her first serious depression; a year later, she experienced a second manic episode.

The Special Nature of Teenage Depression

As we said earlier, a teenager with a severe depression has a lot of the same difficulties as a depressed adult. However, there are differences. One is that younger people seem to be more deeply affected by what is going on around them. Even when depressed, a teenager may be able to have a good time for a little while with a good friend, doing something enjoyable, for instance. After the activity is over, however, the sad feelings will probably return.

Another difference is that sometimes teenagers can put on a front that hides their sadness. Young people hate to feel passive and helpless, and depression causes this. To lessen these feelings, they may become very

17

active, taking risks to make themselves feel more alive. They might react to their depression by being absent from school, using drugs, driving a car recklessly, getting angry with teachers, parents, and friends, fighting, or committing crimes. These actions demand so much attention that others may overlook the depression.

The Number of Depressed Teenagers

It is very difficult to figure out how many young people actually become depressed. As we know, there are many different kinds of depression. There is mild reactive depression, mild chronic depression, major depression, major depression with psychosis, and manic-depression. Some teenagers may have a few symptoms of depression, such as trouble falling asleep or loss of appetite, for a few days. Other teenagers may feel sad from time to time, but have none of the other symptoms. In both adolescents and adults, many more females than males become depressed.

Dr. Hudgens examined all of the teenagers who were hospitalized for psychiatric reasons at Washington University Medical Center. Some 40 percent of these patients had significant depressions. He found that 20 percent of the adolescents who were hospitalized for physical illness also had significant depressions. This points out how stressful it is for a teenager to have serious physical problems that require hospitalization and how frequently depression results.

Of course, most depressions do not lead to hospitalization. Even looking at those teenagers who came for counseling at the Adolescent Health Center at Mount Sinai Medical Center, in New York City, Dr. Richard Wortman, one of the authors of this book, found that mild reactive depressions and mild chronic depressions were two of the three most common problems.

It is clear that many teenagers will have depressions. Some will be severe and others mild. Some will last for years and others for only weeks. Each one of these young people will probably feel very alone at that time. But actually a number of others will be having the same feelings and thoughts. Maybe it can help a depressed teenager feel less different and alone to know this is a common condition shared with other young people.

CHAPTER 2

What Brings It On

Depressions often seem to be caused by a loss. A parent may die, a friend may move away, or the teenager might fail a math test. Any one of these events could lead to a depression. Certainly the most difficult kind of loss is the death of a loved one. It is normal for a period of sadness to follow such a loss. Erich Lindemann, a Harvard Medical School psychiatrist, observed this kind of loss in the relatives of a large number of people killed in a fire at the Coconut Grove, a nightclub in Boston, Massachusetts, in 1943. During this time, the mourners did what Lindemann called "grief work." They freed themselves of the bond to their lost loved ones, readjusted to life without the deceased persons, and began to make new relationships. At the same time, most of these relatives experienced physical distress, constant thoughts about the lost person, guilty feelings about the death, feelings of anger toward the doctors and other medical staff, and a change of behavior, such as restlessness and the inability to get things done or to be socially polite. This condition, which

Lindemann called normal acute grief, lasted from four to six weeks.

Although many of these characteristics were described in Chapter 1 as part of clinical depression, Lindemann found depression in only a small number of the relatives. That a large number of these people did not become seriously depressed indicates that loss alone does not necessarily cause depression.

The Psychology of Depression

The psychoanalyst who first described the difference between depression and normal grief following the loss of a loved one was Karl Abraham. In 1911, he pointed out that the major difference is that mourners are concerned mainly about the lost person, whereas depressed people think about their own feelings of loss, guilt, and low self-esteem. Abraham believed that these negative feelings were the result of the anger felt toward the lost person. Depressed people regard these hostile feelings toward the lost loved one as unacceptable, so they cannot acknowledge them. They redirect the hostility toward themselves. This causes a loss of self-respect. Depressed persons exaggerate their own sins and inadequacies, even though they have no realistic basis.

Depression involves a serious loss of self-esteem. A number of circumstances can lower a person's opinion of himself or herself.

1. A bad family atmosphere can lead to the early development of a poor self-image.

2. Strong ideas of what is right and wrong can lead to guilt and low self-esteem. Even people who are generally good will frequently see themselves as bad.
3. Unreasonably high expectations may lead to repeated failures and result in a loss of self-esteem. People who expect to get the best grade on every test, or who want to be everybody's friend may wind up failing in their own eyes even if they are successful or popular.
4. Children with learning difficulties, physical disabilities, or illnesses are more likely to experience failure and loss of self-esteem.

Sigmund Freud, the father of psychoanalysis, believed that if a parent withholds love and support during the early years of a child's life, the child will be vulnerable to depression later on in life. It is difficult to prove this, however, because so many different things influence a person's life. Most professionals agree that there is no simple relationship between a single early loss and later depression. The quality of family relationships both before and after the loss are also important. Probably long-term deprivation or a series of losses is more damaging than one major loss, if love and support are provided.

Ideally children grow up in an atmosphere of parental love and concern. Such children learn to deal with frustrations and meet challenges, and they will have enough inner strength and parental support to succeed. Self-confidence will grow out of this, which should permit the children to enter into new situations and take on new challenges, without being held back by doubts. These children will develop a sense of right and wrong, but with their parents' love will continue to see themselves as good persons in spite of minor misbehavior. They will therefore be able to assert themselves without inhibitions. As teenagers they should be fairly resistant to depression, even if they suffer a loss.

Adolescent Losses

Some children enter adolescence with a vulnerability to depression produced by either biological factors or early childhood experiences. These teenagers may lack the normal ability to deal with disappointments. Consider how Raphael's early childhood made him prone to depression.

Raphael sits by the window looking down at the traffic in New York City. At 6:30 A.M., traffic is light and the headlights make streaks and flashes through the semidarkness. The hour is unimportant to Raphael. He sleeps poorly and has no place to go. Raphael is sixteen and a dropout. His prospects for the future appear bleak. Although he was born in New York City, he has trouble speaking and reading English. This is because Raphael spent most of his life in Puerto Rico with his grandmother. His mother was only seventeen when Raphael was born. She had no interest in child rearing. When his grandmother died a year ago, Raphael came back to the States to live with his mother. She accepted him reluctantly, because her third husband and a variety of stepbrothers and stepsisters already crowded the small apartment. Raphael feels lonely, has no friends, and longs for the warm climate of Puerto Rico and the sea breezes along the beaches. The loss of a "real" mother early in life and the second loss of the only loving person he ever knew has caused an increasing depression in Raphael. He does not believe that he can survive in this towering, crowded, public housing project. Maybe he'll jump from the seventeenth-floor window.

If an adolescent is unusually sensitive, shy, and retiring, the risk may be further complicated by little or no communication of emotional needs. Because Raphael cannot get his indifferent mother to understand his needs and she fails to recognize the meaning of his withdrawn behavior, Raphael believes that all adults are uncaring. This belief and the sudden loss of his late grandmother have led to increased despair and suicidal fantasies.

Like the death of a loved one, separation and divorce are a loss, too. The family holds the strongest identification for children. Its members provide not only physical and emotional support, but a sense of continuity also. When this is interrupted or suspended by separation or divorce, children may suffer short or long periods of depression. J. D. Wallerstein and J. B. Kelly, authors of *Surviving the Breakup: How Children and Parents Cope with Divorce,* wrote that adolescents, after an initial period of intensive emotional upset, experience and express great anger. They appear to understand the reasons for divorce, but they are often deeply worried about the effects of the separation on their own futures. The divorce of Mark's parents, for example, put additional pressure on his already shaky school situation.

Mark began high school with an unusually high level

of interest in everything. He was the oldest of three children. During his sophomore year, his parents went through a bitter divorce. Mark's father was allowed to visit the children twice a month. As the only boy, Mark was clearly his father's favorite. Mark's mother resented the unequal treatment given to his sisters. So arguments continued, and Mark's father often left the house after twenty minutes. When things went well, Mark accompanied his father on business trips to Los Angeles, Chicago, and Miami, missing several days of school to travel each time he went. These absences resulted in lower grades. In the middle of his junior year, Mark was barely passing. Pressure from his mother to do better and the excuses Mark made to his father gave Mark migraine headaches and periods of depression. Mark had always known that his father expected him to attend Princeton University. But Mark knew he would never graduate with honors from Princeton as his father had.

As the months passed, Mark's grades slipped even lower. He didn't want his father to know that his son was barely passing the modified courses he had chosen. Mark became increasingly depressed, with loss of appetite and sleepless nights. He thought of running away. But he knew that his parents would probably find him. So Mark made excuses to avoid visiting his father.

Adolescents are especially sensitive to the specific aspects of development: physical, psychological, and social. Since most teenagers experience some doubts and fears about themselves and the way others see them, the family is a critical source of support during the adolescent years. If family relations are strained, a teenager may become vulnerable because of the lack of a stabilizing force.

When both parents work, children may be expected to assume a great deal of responsibility. Kayla's predicament is a good example. Kayla's mother is a night nurse, and her father is a police officer who often puts in overtime and has to work alternating shifts. As the oldest of four children, Kayla has to care for her brothers and sister. While her mother sleeps, Kayla prepares dinner. Afterwards, she cleans up and helps the younger ones with their homework. Before she can begin her own homework, Kayla has to put the children to bed and make the next day's lunches for everyone. Sometimes Kayla may be found doing the family laundry as late as 11:30 P.M. She feels that her mother demands too much from her, but Kayla suppresses her anger and hurt feelings.

Frequently Kayla finds it difficult to follow the teachers' lessons, and she has been reprimanded for falling asleep in class. When Kayla complains about the heavy work load, her mother says, "When I was your age . . ." Kayla wonders how long she can continue. Although her family is intact, with a mother and a father, Kayla feels that her parents have deserted her. She works hard to please them. She loves them and needs their love, but she feels that they do not love and support her. Her depression, however, prevents her from improving her situation.

A parent may be present in the home, but because of his or her own problems may not be able to provide love and care consistently to the children. If parents become depressed, they may withdraw from their children. For the child, this may be just as painful as if the parents were not there at all. This can also happen when there is a serious or prolonged illness in a family.

Perhaps the situation in the Costello family shows this. Mrs. Costello has diabetes, complicated by a serious heart ailment. She spends most of her time in bed. Oxygen helps her to breathe. Peter, the oldest boy of the five children, does most of the child rearing, household tasks, and shopping. At sixteen, he is a good cook, too. Mrs. Costello is cared for partly by her husband, who works nights. During the day, he takes his wife to clinics, doctors, and agencies. Peter feels deserted by both parents, since his mother's illness leaves little time for Peter to develop a sense of family with them. They are overwhelmed by Mrs. Costello's special diets, injections, exercises, and medication. Peter feels angry and depressed at times and resents the loss of both parents' love and attention.

Just as teenagers remain dependent on parents, they also look to other adults, such as teachers and coaches, for approval, if not love. A harsh word from a coach or a poor grade on an English paper can also seem like a great loss.

Miss Waters was Joshua's favorite teacher. Although he wasn't the smartest student in English class, Josh tried to do passing work. Often his essays were poorly organized, contained many grammatical errors, and were dull. He wrote about his interests—the early West, wild animals, and African tribal warfare. Josh's enthusiasm far exceeded his talents, however. His efforts were returned with Miss Waters' comments and corrections written in red across the pages.

Josh's eagerness to improve and thus gain the approval of Miss Waters caused him to be unethical.

Joshua cheated. At the local library, he found a scholarly report written by a noted historian. Josh copied it carefully on lined paper and signed his own name. Unfortunately for Josh, Miss Waters recognized the work immediately. Her disappointment caused Josh much pain and embarrassment. Josh felt terrible. He had no excuse for his actions. His loss of self-respect was painful. Miss Waters' affection and praise were lost to him forever.

Social acceptance and approval by peers also has an increasingly important effect on a teenager's self-esteem. Rejection by a friend or a club is one more possible source of loss. Formal and informal groups and cliques spring up naturally in schools. Being in the right crowd appears to be more important in some schools than in others. Where it is important, this exclusiveness can cause anxiety and tension, especially to those who don't make it.

At every high school, one club or activity seems to have exalted status. Those fortunate enough to belong to that group are treated with adoration and admiration reserved for royalty. Other students envy them or court their favor, hoping some of the glory will reflect on them.

At some schools, the quarterback is the hero. At others, it is the head cheerleader or the highest-scoring basketball player or a hot saxophone soloist. In still other schools, the members of a certain club are the heroes and social leaders.

Failure in academic work, sports, dance, drama, or some other activity may lead to the loss of a hoped-for future goal. For example, a teenager may have to give up the idea of being a mathematician, a professional basketball player, or an actress. Some teenagers experience this loss as a significant trauma.

DOWN IS NOT OUT

The loss is even more painful when well-meaning parents attempt to fulfill their broken dreams and aspirations through their children. Toby's parents, particularly his father, were certain that their son would be a professional football player. Toby was a well-developed six-footer at the age of twelve. He also liked playing football. Toby's mother fed him high-energy foods, extra vitamins, and minerals. His father attended every practice session of Toby's team. Both watched over Toby's health and welfare with extraordinary dedication. Toby practiced twelve months a year, but he was just another team player—he had no potential to be a superstar. The coach broke the news as gently as possible to the devastated parents; their Toby would never be another Joe Namath. Toby felt that his entire future had been wiped out. Football was his only reason for living. Self-doubts and a loss of self-respect followed.

One more kind of loss will be mentioned here, because it has a major impact on a teenager's sense of well-being. It is the loss of physical health. Chronic, or prolonged, illness is particularly hard for teenagers to accept. This will be discussed in more detail in Chapter 3. But learning about Donny's battle with polio will give some understanding of what it is like.

Donny has had home teachers since he was seven years old. Most were kind, patient, and helpful. But Donny missed going to school with other kids. He often looked at his long, thin legs encased in heavy braces and felt self-pity and disgust. Why me? he would wonder. He would never play baseball, football, or handball with his brothers. Donny's weak shoulders and arms prevented him from using crutches. He would spend the rest of his life in a wheelchair. For eight years, Donny's mother devised puzzles, games, and comic books that allowed Donny to participate with the family in interesting leisure activities. But Donny's future looked gloomy. At fifteen, when most kids were enjoying high school and looking forward to college, Donny could only sit and stare out of the window, watching the world pass him by.

Loss and Depression

Although a number of losses can set off a depression in adolescence, there is no convincing scientific evidence of a connection between life stresses and a sustained depression. On the other hand, the connection has not been disproved either. Recent studies by Dr. Hudgens and his co-workers have demonstrated that stress contributes to the worsening of psychological disorders that are already present. However, this is different from proving that loss can produce such a disorder in a completely healthy individual. Even so, most psychiatrists and researchers, based on their clinical and research experience, believe that a loss can often lead to a depression. A number of other poorly understood circumstances—either past experiences or genetic tendencies—can make a person vulnerable to such stress.

Genetic Contribution to Depression

There is strong support for the role that genetics plays in the occurrence of major depressions. In other words, parents can transmit to their children an increased possibility of depression. To understand the genetic and biological aspects of depression, you must be familiar with some technical terms. You do not need to have a prior knowledge of these fields to understand what follows, but you must read carefully.

One way that researchers study the effect of genetic transmission is to examine identical or fraternal twins. Identical twins come from the same egg and therefore have identical genes. Fraternal twins come from two separate eggs and have only some of the same genes. They may look something alike, as brothers and sisters often do, but they are not identical in appearance. If there is a significant genetic contribution to major depressions, you would expect that if one twin has depressions, then there would be an increased occurrence of depression in the other twin as well. This should happen more frequently in identical twins who have identical genes than in fraternal twins, who don't.

One study was done with thirty-eight pairs of twins, where one twin had experienced a major depression. The identical twins had a 57 percent concordance rate (the tendency for both twins to develop a depression), and fraternal twins had a 29 percent concordance rate. These percentages are what researchers would predict with genetic transmission. The greater the similarity in genes, the higher the concordance rate.

Each set of twins was raised in the same environment, and this might have played a significant role in the development of depression. To test the effects of environment, another study was done with twelve pairs of identical twins who were raised apart from each other. In eight of the twelve pairs, both twins had depression. This gives a concordance rate of about 67 percent, in spite of the fact that each of the twins was raised in a different home.

There is also a lot of evidence that depression occurs in families, and particularly that children with depression symptoms have parents with depression. Michael Strober, a psychologist at the University of California at Los Angeles, found that the risk of depression in parents of depressed adolescents was 3.5 times greater than with parents of nondepressed adolescents. It is possible that part of the explanation for this high rate of depression in the parents of depressed adolescents is environmental. But in another study of the familial occurrence of depression, Myrna Weissman of Yale Medical School was able to factor out the significance of environmental factors that could have resulted from the parent's illness. This indicates that the frequent occurrence of depression in some families is based on heredity, apart from a stressful home situation. Together, these studies make a strong argument for the genetic transmission of depression.

The specific genes and chromosomes involved in this transmission and the nature of the biological vulnerability that the genes cause are not well understood. With this knowledge, it would be possible to better treat and even to prevent some kinds of depression.

The Physical Aspects of Depression

Let's start with a question: If depression is a psychological disorder, why are we talking about physical aspects? One reason is that the physical and the psychological are connected through the nervous system and the endocrine system. Second, if you look closely at the symptoms of a major depression, you'll see that the physical aspects are quite striking. Some of the ones mentioned in Chapter 1 were loss of appetite, sleeping difficulty, and tiredness. In addition to these, nausea, chest and back pain, stomachache, diarrhea, constipation, and muscle aches are all found more frequently in depressed adolescents than in nondepressed ones.

In addition to looking at the obvious symptoms of depression, some researchers have found other less obvious physical aspects of depression. They have shown that a significant number of depressed children, adolescents, and adults secrete more cortisol than nondepressed people. Cortisol is a steroid produced by the adrenal gland, which is part of the endocrine system. It has been found that 50 percent of adults with a disease where there is an overproduction of cortisol (adrenal hyperplasis) have severe depressive symptoms.

Along with difficulty in sleeping, other sleep patterns have also been studied in depressed people. A phase of sleep where the sleeper has rapid eye movements is called REM sleep. This seems to be the time when most dreams occur. In depressed adults and adolescents, REM sleep begins much sooner after falling asleep than it does in people who are not depressed. Also, the number of eye movements per minute of REM sleep is significantly greater in depressed adults and adolescents. These facts demonstrate the physical aspects of depression.

The Biological Basis of Depression

The actual biological (physical) basis of depression is not completely understood. Much attention has been directed at the chemical compounds that are responsible for the transmission of messages from one nerve to the next in the central nervous system. The nerves, or neurons, are constantly being charged and discharged in the process of transmitting messages. Since the neurons are separated from each other by a small space, called a synapse, the charges must be carried across this space to stimulate the neighboring neuron. Chemical compounds called neurotransmitters carry these charges. It is generally believed that an increase in these neurotransmitters leads to overactivity and alertness and the clinical state of mania, and that a decrease leads to sedation, inactivity, and depression.

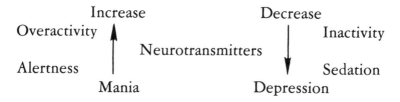

There are two good reasons to believe that a connection exists between the level of neurotransmitters and depression and mania:

1. Drugs that reduce the brain's neurotransmitters cause depression.
2. Drugs that are effective in the treatment of depression increase the level of available neurotransmitters in the brain.

This sounds quite simple, but there are a number of different kinds of neurotransmitters, and the biochemical changes in depression and mania are probably most complex. As we mentioned, increased cortisol also seems to be associated with depression. It is interesting that the secretion of a number of hormones produced by the endocrine system is controlled by neurons, which in turn are activated by neurotransmitters. We don't know whether the increased cortisol secretion is a general response to stress or a cause of the depression itself. Much research is being done in this area, and we may be able to answer these questions in the future.

Even now we can understand some of the causes of depression. It is possible that a biological vulnerability to depression is inherited through one's genes. Early experiences in life, such as losses, frustrations, and prolonged stress, may increase that inherited vulnerability. Later on in life, an additional trauma may set off a combined biological and psychological depression with both physical and psychological symptoms. When there is a strong biological vulnerability, a person may develop a depression even without early life traumas or loss. In some instances, when everything is going well, a person may, for no apparent reason, become severely depressed.

CHAPTER 3

Doing Forty in the Fast Lane

The accelerated growth, the desire to leap with giant steps into adulthood, and a rapidly changing body coupled with parental and legal restraints often make adolescents feel that they are doing forty in the fast lane. Many teenagers find much of what is happening to their bodies acceptable but uncomfortable at times—the big feet, long, skinny legs, awkward gait, budding breasts, voracious appetitie, and changing voices. During adolescence an increase in depression occurs. Although some biological factors may be involved, there are many psychological aspects of adolescence that may contribute to this increasing occurrence of depression.

Losses during Adolescence

We have described how a loss can set off a depression. What begins as a loss of a loved one becomes the loss of self-esteem in a depressed person. Adolescence is a time when a person longs for independence, a mature sexual identity, intimate personal relations, and autonomy. To achieve these goals, the teenager must first give up or lose several things that have provided him or her with a great deal of security throughout childhood:

1. In childhood, the body grows slowly in size, strength, and agility and is comfortably the child's own. In comparison, the teenager's body begins to grow rapidly and to show a number of dramatic sexual changes. The body may actually feel foreign to a teenager.

2. Teenagers must give up their dependence on parents whom they have always seen as generally right, powerful, wise, loving, and available. Adolescents begin to put some emotional distance between themselves and their parents. They also begin to view their parents more realistically; parents do not always appear right, wise, and powerful. Both of these circumstances lead to the loss of the security that existed during childhood.

3. In childhood, a person has a clear-cut knowledge of right and wrong based on parents' values. These standards are fairly easy to uphold and do not prevent a child from having a good time. In adolescence, however, the teenagers may become aware of different and conflicting value systems that do not always provide clear-cut guidelines for behavior. He or she may also have some strong aggressive and sexual feelings and the urge to act upon them, knowing that to do so will get him or her into trouble and cause guilty feelings.

4. Children can expect to succeed at whatever they try to do: throw a ball, learn to spell, or use a computer. Their future goals can range from being a dancer to becoming an astronaut and need not be realistically based on any capabilities or skills. Teenagers also may set idealistic and unattainable goals. When they realize they are not likely to reach their objectives, they may become discouraged and disappointed. If they do not get high grades at school, for example, they worry that they will not get into prestigious colleges.

All of this security is vital for the younger child, but it imposes limitations on the developing teenager, who must give it up in order to continue to grow. This security, however, is often lost before there is a ready replacement for it. So the teenager loses the comfortable body, the dependent relationship with powerful parents, the simple parental value system, and the expectations of success.

A similar situation exists at an earlier stage in life. Young toddlers hold their parents' hands when learning how to walk, but at some point both the children and their parents must let go. This creates some uncertainty. There will most likely be some falls and some bumps with some tears. Parents can comfort their children and help them stand up, but the toddlers must let go and practice alone in order to gain their balance. When children fall, they may feel as though they have been abandoned; they become painfully aware of their own limitations and their need for parental help. The adolescent will also have feelings of inadequacy, insecurity, and abandonment. It is then that the loss of childhood security may lead to a loss of self-esteem and increase the risk of depression. Don experienced much of this as he tried to stand on his own.

Although Don was doing well in school, held a part-time job, and did volunteer tutoring, his parents still saw him as that cuddly little curly-haired boy. "Please don't call me Donnie! And don't wait up for me," he yelled at them in frustration. "I can handle it." Like any learner, Don made mistakes, some major ones. Once he got involved in a ticket-scalping scheme. Don offered to sell tickets to the football game on Thanksgiving Day. He believed the fast-talking confidence men who told him that the $25 ticket price included a $10 donation to the Children's Hospital. Another time, Don attempted to capture two armed intruders who were methodically looting his family's house. For his heroism, Don spent three weeks in the hospital recuperating from a severe beating. And then last summer, Don invested his entire savings of $800 in a worthless roundworm farm. Don's father was angry, because Don hadn't consulted him. Don's mother accused her husband of not being aware of what was happening to their son.

Their criticism only made Don more rebellious and frustrated. He broke curfew and missed dinner with the family. The parents' refusal to allow Don to grow at his own pace caused a breakdown in communications and made the whole family unhappy. But a near tragedy turned things around. Don, a strong swimmer, rescued two young children who had ventured too far from the shores of a pond. The whole story was reported in the local newspaper with accompanying photographs, and the mayor presented Don with a brass plaque for bravery. Don became a local hero. Pride in their son and recognition of his maturity led the parents to fully accept Don as a growing, responsible, and sincere adolescent. Don had adjusted to the loss of childhood security and was functioning on his own.

A Developing Sexual Body

The most striking and profound changes of early adolescence are biological, or physical. These are related to the endocrine changes of puberty and affect almost every system of the body, including height, facial contours, fat distribution, muscular development, sexual characteristics, reproductive capacity, and energy levels. These changes have a striking effect on all other aspects of a person's development. The age at which these biological changes occur varies greatly and can make a big difference on their psychosocial impact. A girl may have her first period (menarche) at any age between nine and sixteen. In the same junior high school classroom, one boy may be physically mature, with a beard, pubic hair, broad muscular shoulders, and a large penis, while a classmate of the same age may not yet have begun to experience these changes. A third classmate will be somewhere in between. This is particularly true of students in junior high school, grades seven to nine.

Being Different

Because these changes occur rapidly and are dramatic and far-reaching in nature, young adolescents may be very self-conscious, if not downright uncomfortable, with their bodies. This discomfort can be caused by changes that make a teenager feel different, such as a long nose, hairy legs, heavy thighs, or big breasts. Or the self-consciousness may be caused by the lack of such changes. When everyone else is becoming more physically mature, it is hard for the one or two boys or girls who continue to look like little children. Teenagers look to one another for acceptance and approval. Their parents' compliments on a new hairstyle or jacket are no longer enough. In the words of one fourteen-year-old girl, "My mother would say I was pretty no matter what I looked like. That's what parents are supposed to do. If I really want to find out how I look, I have to ask a friend."

The need to be similar to peers affects all aspects of a teenager's life. The boy or girl who likes music or movies that are generally not popular is made to feel uncomfortably different. The fourteen-year-old boy whose favorite music is the Bach B-Minor Mass will have trouble fitting into most groups. If one teenager's curfew is much earlier than others', he or she will feel uncomfortably different. Some parents may enforce dress codes for their teenage children that make them look different from their peers. One fifteen-year-old boy had a group of friends who all wore black leather jackets. His parents did not want their son to look "punk," and they refused to buy him one or permit him to save money and purchase one for himself. Although the boy was generally popular and well liked by his friends, he felt uncomfortably different without that black leather jacket.

The Importance of Personal Appearance

A majority of teenagers feel uncomfortable about some aspect of their appearance, girls more so than boys. Why are girls more likely to be dissatisfied with their looks? First, more attention is paid to a girl's appearance than to a boy's. If a girl is not considered pretty, she may not be popular. But a boy need not be particularly handsome to be accepted by both other boys and girls. The second circumstance that makes things harder for girls is the rigid standards of female beauty personified by models and popular, glamorous actresses. A premium is placed on being tall, slender, and full-breasted. The majority of girls are not made that way, and no amount of dieting or exercising can change that fact. The amount of concern that this unattainable ideal causes is attested to by the fact that most teenage girls go on weight-losing diets at some time. Although other factors are also involved, one of the causes of anorexia nervosa is the preoccupation with thinness among girls and women. A girl who is a little overweight, or even of normal weight and just big-boned, may be considered unattractive and fat by peers and herself. This is unfortunate, especially during adolescence when peer acceptance and approval are so important.

Early Developing Girls

Because girls generally begin to mature about two years before boys, the first couple of girls in a class who reach puberty may draw a lot of attention from their peers. Attention can be a positive and desirable thing, but most ten- or eleven-year-old girls are not ready for the kind of attention they receive. Michelle, an eleven-year-old, described how the boys would whistle at her and try to "feel her up," by bumping into her developing breasts. She said that she tried to ignore them, but admitted that this was very hard to do. She felt generally protected and safe when in school, but after school the attention she received from the boys was not monitored or controlled by teachers. She felt very self-conscious and somewhat threatened. Instead of playing outside after school, as she had at an earlier age, Michelle would go directly home to read. She felt a little lonely. The other girls in her class who had not yet started to develop sexually also seemed to maintain some distance from Michelle. This added to her feeling of isolation and to her concern that something might be wrong with her.

Parents might also feel uncomfortable with their daughter's developing sexuality. A father who was once quite close and affectionate may seem to draw away as his daughter grows older. A mother may find herself a little jealous of her daughter's emerging sexual maturity, beauty, and youth. This can lead to some competitiveness, producing tension and distance between the two of them. Both parents may restrict their daughter to protect her from young men's sexual advances. For the girl who has been given increasing freedom and responsibility as she got older, this sudden imposition of rules and regulations will be unwelcome. She will not only see them as unreasonable restraints, but will also feel that her parents lack confidence in her. The message she receives is that the world is unsafe, that she cannot take care of herself, and that her parents don't trust her. This may cause the girl to question her own worth and to lose some of her self-esteem. If she rebels against her parents, she may experience guilt.

Late Developing Girls

Girls who are late developers may also have some specific concerns, although they generally have less difficulty than the early developer. Even at an older age, they will be seen as younger girls and will probably not have many social opportunities because of their appearance. The interest that boys show in girls is a source of self-esteem, and late-developing girls will miss some of this. Well-intentioned parents can make things worse by focusing too much attention on late but normal sexual development. Many mothers take perfectly normal adolescent girls to the doctor if they do not have their first period by a certain age. Even though most doctors will assure them that the girls are totally normal, this parental concern and medical intervention may cause a girl to feel different and self-conscious.

It is not surprising that girls who feel most comfortable and positive about their physical and sexual maturity are generally those whose age of development is somewhere in the middle. These girls seem to be ready for bodily changes and the associated sexual and social demands. Their friends and parents also seem to be ready for and comfortable with their growing up. These girls are less likely to feel different and isolated, with a loss of self-esteem, than either their earlier or later developing peers.

Late Developing Boys

For boys, it is the late developer who runs the greatest risk of having a negative self-concept and being rejected by his group. Adolescent males generally gain respect if they are big, strong, and athletic. Late developing boys find it difficult to excel in sports that require physical maturity and size, like football and basketball. These are the glamorous sports that receive the most attention from peers.

Being underdeveloped in comparison to peers can be a source of intense embarrassment. One academically capable thirteen-year-old boy was truant one day a week. He missed every Thursday, which was the day he was scheduled for gym class. He was not too concerned by his lack of athletic ability, but as a late developer, he was the only boy without pubic hair. He also thought his penis was smaller than every other boy's. The others kidded him about his appearance, and he tried to avoid this by changing into his gym shorts very quickly in one corner of the locker room. This attracted more attention to him, because most of the other guys were horsing around undressed. Some of the kidding became cruel, as they called him a sissy and a faggot. He was neither, but was unwilling to fight to prove it. The boy's solution was to avoid the situation by staying at home on gym-class day. This increased his negative feelings about himself and his isolation from the other boys.

Late developing boys often become the object of teasing. Although the other boys may not intend to really hurt him, once a boy is labeled a "faggot," he may find it hard to accept and feel good about himself. Frank was always the smallest kid in his class. When the students lined up, he was first. At fourteen, he was the only short boy in a class of giants. At school dances, Frank served punch and cookies or worked in the cloakroom. He learned how to dance by watching the other kids. Frank didn't have the nerve to ask a girl to dance. Most of them were much taller than he was anyway. His size kept him off varsity teams, too. He was too short for basketball, too small for football, and too weak for tennis. His need to be wanted and appreciated by his peers was great. This loss of affiliation caused him to withdraw into a mild depression. When he was sixteen, Frank turned to swimming and track at his coach's insistence. By graduation, Frank had won several medals. Although he would never be tall, Frank found ways to express his uniqueness in a positive and satisfying way, which gained the admiration and acceptance of his peers.

Early Developing Boys

It is clearly an advantage for a boy to mature early. He captures the interest of the girls, many of whom start to mature before the boys. This attention from the girls also adds to his prestige in the eyes of other boys. In addition, his physical prowess is superior to that of his less developed peers. He is more likely to be chosen as a leader and will generally gain in self-confidence and self-esteem.

DOWN IS NOT OUT

A major complication may occur, however, if the boy's expectations far exceed his capabilities. Some big, strong boys are neither agile nor athletic. This may disappoint the boy, his peers, his coaches, and even his parents. There is pressure for well-developed boys to compete in sports and, if they don't, they may be disillusioned and may also feel that they have disappointed others.

When John was thirteen years old, he stood six feet two inches tall and weighed 200 pounds. He was the best basketball and football player his age on Staten Island. He received offers of sports scholarship from prep schools, but his real interest was dramatics, and none of the schools had a good drama program. In addition, he would have little time for dramatics after football and basketball practice. He decided to accept one of these scholarships and to continue to play ball, but he felt he was compromising himself and giving up something that was more important to him than sports.

In some neighborhoods, boys must be willing to fight to maintain the respect of their peers. Although the strong and big boys may be best equipped to do this, they are also more frequently attacked by others who are trying to prove how tough they are. One unusually tall sixteen-year-old was often singled out by competing gangs of youths. If he avoided the fight or was beaten, his entire group of friends would be discredited. Although he took some pride in this position of leadership, he was also frightened and at times did not really want to fight. He was saddened by his own aggressive behavior, although he saw no choice in the matter.

Some of the most uncomfortable expectations occur in fatherless homes. A big, mature, but young teenager

48

may be expected to become the protector of the family. Because of his size, his mother may want him to take the missing father's place. If he feels that he can't measure up to the task and tries to avoid the responsibility, he may be criticized. When he does attempt to assert some authority, his younger brothers and sisters may resent him and behave angrily and disrespectfully toward him. Whichever he does, he loses in some way and feels bad about himself. In other homes, a young person may have to assume responsibility for the entire family, because there is no one else to do it. He is burdened with the tremendous task of being father, older brother, and substitute husband. What happened to Angel Garcia shows how impossible things can get.

Angel Garcia silently cursed the security guard who glared at him across the dimly lit hotel lobby. Angel had been warned three times not to sit on the soiled, broken-down sofa. It was nineteen months now and still the end was not in sight. Nineteen months is a long time to be without a home, a bed, a refrigerator. Six people crowded into two small hotel rooms—Angel, four brothers and sisters, and their ailing mother. Before the fire had destroyed their Bronx apartment, there had been lots of good times. How Angel longed to be back on Trinity Avenue.

Angel left the hotel and walked several blocks to Bryant Park. There had been a recent public outcry against the pushers and addicts who infested the park. People walked through there only during the daytime. Even then it was risky. Today several artists were hanging up their paintings on a collapsible screen. A young woman sat before an easel sketching in charcoal. Her subject was a grinning, toothless derelict. A half-empty wine bottle protruded from the pocket of his torn, filthy pants. For attracting the crowd of bystanders and potential customers, the artist would give this wretched creature a couple of dollars, enough to buy several bottles of cheap wine. As Angel stared at the pathetic figure, tears filled his eyes. Would he become a reject of society, too?

After a supper of beans, rice, and chicken backs eaten with plastic forks off paper plates, Angel settled the younger children in front of the television set in the other bedroom. His mother, an asthmatic, sat propped up on the double bed. Although the windows were open, she had difficulty breathing. Tomorrow morning, she would go to the clinic for her weekly visit while Angel watched the children. Angel sat on the bed and held his mother's moist, hot hand. What will happen to the family if she is hospitalized or if she dies?, Angel thought to himself. Hot tears streamed down his face.

Over the next few days, Angel tried to find work. He was unsuccessful. Hungry, tired, and dejected, he returned to the hotel each night increasingly depressed. Nothing seemed to be working for him.

Angel attended three schools within eighteen months. He went to one in the middle of the term, too late to register for courses he needed. Three months later, the Garcias were moved to a motel in Newark, New Jersey. When Angel attempted to enroll in the tenth grade there, the assistant principal wanted all of his primary school records. "They're in the mail" was the only response Angel could get from his many telephone calls to school secretaries. When the Garcias were moved back to Manhattan, Angel was relieved. He hoped he could return to school and see some of his friends. But the bureaucracy of the large school system had swallowed up his records.

Lonely for his friends and the old neighborhood, frustrated and angry at the large, indifferent system of administering education, welfare, and health services to citizens, Angel felt betrayed and trapped. He stopped trying to return to school or get a job. He stopped eating. Angel stayed inside the old welfare hotel. Each day, he sat quietly in one of the rooms, appearing to be unconcerned about the flies, mice, and cockroaches around him, but becoming increasingly depressed and withdrawn.

A week later, the ambulance came to take his mother to Bellevue Hospital. She was having an acute asthmatic attack. The paramedics picked up the almost unconscious teenager and took him, too.

During the rapid growth and development of adolescence, physical maturity sometimes outdistances psychological development. This can produce an energetic but disorganized individual who may have spontaneous and unpredictable highs and lows. One low may mark the onset of a depression, which can be initiated by a loss. In order to move toward independence, the adolescent must lose or give up some of the security he or she enjoyed as a child. The adolescent must also learn to cope with sexual changes and a variety of value systems. Some adolescents develop earlier or later than others. Some must contend with expectations that cannot be fulfilled. All of these circumstances entail loss and may lead to depression.

CHAPTER 4

I'd Rather Do It Myself

Today's society encourages children to seek autonomy, separation from their parents, independence. Their upbringing is laced with permissive principles, making them open, unashamed, and not guilt-ridden. Adults miss the quiet, well-mannered, obedient children of past eras, however. With those passive children, the adults felt less threatened, more secure in their positions of control. But history has revealed the many negative effects of a repressed childhood. So parents often find themselves in a dilemma. What is too little or too much control?

Adolescence is a time for trying out behavior. Teenagers experiment with different life-styles, choices of friends, relationships with the opposite sex. Some have values quite different from those of their parents, often choosing to adopt the values of their peer group.

Because their need to experiment is so strong, adolescents view the restrictions placed on them by parents, school, and society as a lack of trust in them. They may feel this way even when they know that some of their behavior is wrong or dangerous. The result sometimes shows itself in rebellious, hostile behavior, as they try to cope with the demands put on a rapidly developing body and a slowly evolving new identity.

But it is not true that teenagers must be openly rebellious toward their parents in order to grow into normal independent adults. Most young people generally trust their parents and continue to look to them for approval throughout their teenage years. Naturally, disagreements occur regarding clothes, hairstyles, and curfews. These discussions can become heated. These disagreements show the increasing influence of peers and the importance of life outside the home. Teenagers work hard to master the rest of their world. To do this, they must let go of their parents. The need for parents remains, however, and the adolescents sometimes long to be dependent. Because this longing may seem like a threat to their independence, teenagers may move aggressively away from parents to fight this pull. One way of accomplishing this is to challenge parents' rules and values. Another way is to look at parents' shortcomings so as to discredit them. Either way, the parents are devalued. Younger children see their parents in an idealized way, but teenagers have the mental capacity and the psychological need to see them as less than perfect. This process, called the deidealization of parents, is normal.

Some parents get upset when teenagers challenge their ideas, values, and authority. To them, it may seem like an attack, and parents may become defensive and counterattack or withdraw. By doing so, they may lose the emotional closeness between them and their teenagers. This may be a relief for those teenagers who felt the uncomfortable pull of dependency. Unfortunately, it also leads to feelings of loss and insecurity. In response to these uncomfortable feelings, the young people may try hard to replace their parents with friends. This is why it is important for younger teenagers to have a best friend who can be trusted and who is always there in time of need. It is difficult for them to share this one friend, in the same way that it was difficult for them to share their parents with brothers and sisters. They want to have this person all to themselves so that they can feel secure. Unfortunately, best friends sometimes do leave and find other friends, or they may move away. Then the teenager's feelings of security are temporarily lost. This kind of loss can lead to feelings of abandonment and loss of self-esteem. This happened to two best friends.

Kate and Alison were the best of friends, as close as any thirteen-year-old girls could be. They became friends at camp when they were eleven. Their birthdays were a week apart, and they always planned joint celebrations. Recently, a new family moved into their neighborhood. There was an attractive, thirteen-year-old named Sue in the family. Kate noticed that things began to change between her and Alison when Sue appeared on the scene. Alison still spends a lot of time with Kate. But when they are together all Kate hears is "Sue this" and "Sue that." Kate is hurt and feels that Alison has deserted her for someone prettier and smarter. Kate has lost the snug, warm feeling of a close friendship, and her self-esteem is lowered by her loss. Now she must find a new friend.

A fourteen- to sixteen-year-old teenager will begin to depend on a group of friends for security and identification rather than on one special friend. There are two advantages to this: it is easier to maintain ties with a number of people, and there is less chance of losing all of them at the same time. The old saying, "Don't put all of your eggs in one basket," comes to mind. The need to conform to the group's standards becomes important, though, and that is the disadvantage of this stage of adolescence. If everyone in the group is skipping school and smoking marijuana, for example, it is difficult for one teenager to behave differently and still remain a part of the group. When choices such as this arise, insecure, dependent teenagers are likely to compromise their values for the sake of keeping their friends. This is a no-win situation. Both "bad" behavior, with its accompanying guilt, and "good" behavior, resulting in the loss of friends, will lead to a decrease in self-esteem.

This bleak, no-win situation is not the norm, fortunately. Many parents are able to maintain close, warm relationships with their teenage children, even as they move away emotionally. When this happens, a young person is not likely to behave in a self-destructive way in order to keep friends. Although many teenagers may toy with truancy or marijuana and other drug use out of curiosity and the need to feel independent, they also care enough about themselves and have enough control to refuse to let these activities get out of hand and become destructive. True friends will watch out for one another and discourage types of behavior that are foolish or dangerous.

Values and Behavior

One of the most exciting things about the teenage years is the increasing ability to think in a way that was not possible before. For the first time the whole world of ideas, ideals, and ideologies becomes available. This new kind of thinking is called abstract thinking or formal operational thinking. It allows a person not just to have an idea but to think about that idea in relation to other ideas, to compare and contrast these different ideas. As we have pointed out, teenagers do not automatically accept parental values as their own. They learn to see their parents' value system as one of many value systems. Different religions, different societies, different cultures, different families, and different people all have somewhat different values. For this reason, a certain type of behavior such as swearing may be acceptable in one situation but not in another. Stealing is wrong, but stealing medicine to save the life of a poor sick person may be acceptable in some cultures.

Sex

Sexual behavior and values probably produce more uncertainty, confusion, doubts, discomfort, and guilt than any other area of a young person's life. There are so many conflicting attitudes about making out, having sex, becoming pregnant, having a baby, or having an abortion.

Teenagers are very much aware of the development of their sexual urges. How they cope with their sexual feelings during adolescence will set a pattern for future sexual behavior. Scientists have found that, in general, adolescents are not afraid of their sexuality. Seven out of ten teenagers stated that they liked the recent changes in their bodies. Girls and boys strongly rejected the statement that their bodies were poorly developed, and both groups indicated a relatively smooth transition to emerging sexuality. A majority of the subjects stated that having a friend of the opposite sex was important to them.

Several circumstances can push or pull a teenager into a sexual relationship. First, once the biological changes of puberty have occurred, a strong sexual drive does exist. Second, with the movement away from parents, a teenager may feel some emotional need for closeness. Bringing sexual intercourse into a relationship with a friend may be an attempt to regain the security and closeness that one has lost. Third, with many peers talking about having sex, it may appear to be the thing to do. As they move through their teenage years, boys come to see their virginity as a lack of masculinity. Girls also feel increasing pressure with each year to have sex with boys whom they care about.

Much of the pressure to have or not have sex comes not from teenagers themselves, but from movies and television, say professionals in sex education. Many love stories begin or end in bed. Adolescents confuse sexual attraction and passion with love. What most experience is infatuation.

It is very likely that this is one area where parents' rules are more conservative than their children's behavior. This is not to say that some parents have not had early sexual experience, but what they teach and preach to their children is that later is better and early is bad. The pressures to have sex and the prohibitions against having sex cause many teenagers to have sex and feel guilty about it. This results in a loss of self-esteem.

Expectations and Accomplishments

Teenagers are often accused of being too idealistic. As they become increasingly capable of thinking in terms of ideas and ideals, teenagers begin to hope that they can do things that are bigger and better than what their parents have done. They may want to be more honest, more true to their values, more giving, and more successful in some way. It is hard to accomplish this all of the time. They might do very well for a while, but there are always temporary setbacks. John, a sixteen-year-old, prides himself on his commitment to his fellow man. He wants to be a medical researcher and find the cure for cancer. At times, however, he behaves selfishly. He may turn his back on a friend who needs help in preparing for an exam, for instance. This makes John feel disappointed in himself because he has not lived up to his own ideals.

The increase in mental capacity that makes it possible for teenagers to handle abstract ideas also makes it possible for them to project themselves realistically into the future. This allows them to judge the possibility of attaining future goals. A ten-year-old may envision a career as a scientist each time he or she looks into a microscope. An eleven-year-old who finds an Indian arrowhead sees a future as an archaeologist. A nine-year-old who does a cartwheel immediately becomes an Olympic gymnast. But things are not so easy for the sixteen-year-old who hopes to play professional football or become a ballerina or a doctor. The teenager becomes very aware of the physical and mental requirements, luck, hard work, and money that are needed to achieve success. A teenager who has to give up some of these hopes because of realistic limitations will frequently feel a sense of loss.

Chronic Physical Illness and Depression

A significant number of teenagers with chronic illness and other disabilities become depressed. Some of these long-term illnesses are familiar to you: cerebral palsy, arthritis, heart disease, diabetes, mental retardation, blindness, and the crippling that results from accidents and burns. Depression among the chronically ill or disabled is not surprising when you consider that the developmental tasks of adolescence clash directly with the effects of chronic illness and its treatment. To a young person who is dealing with puberty, physical illness is a threat to both sexuality and body image. Appearing similar to peers and fitting in with them are important, and the ill teenager is faced with the stress of being different and the fear of not being accepted. During a time when there are strong drives toward independence, the stress of illness can lead an adolescent to wish for security and to long to be cared for. Overprotective parents can worsen this conflict.

Chronic illness may actually delay the onset of puberty. This delay may add to the sense of physical inadequacy produced by the illness, especially for boys. Pubertal change brings increase in size, muscle strength, and physical prowess. When these are lacking, boys receive less peer respect and suffer loss of self-esteem.

They are often unable to compete in sports, and this, too, lowers their self-esteem.

Some treatments produce obvious physical side effects. The steroid medication prescribed for severe asthma, for example, causes a teenager's cheeks to become fat and produces a hump between the shoulderblades. If a teenager feels very dependent on peer approval, such differences can damage self-respect.

In later adolescence, the process of making commitments to long-term relationships and setting vocational goals begins. The physical limitations imposed by a chronic illness can have an ill effect on both of these. Some parents encourage their children to hide their illness from potential mates. This just reinforces the teenagers' view of themselves as damaged and undesirable. Some vocational goals will be unattainable as a result of the physical limitations of chronic illness. For some teenagers, the awareness of a shortened life span becomes real for the first time. Distress and depression are understandably common.

The teenage years are striking in how much is gained. Teenagers experience growth in size, strength, agility, sexual capability, and intelligence. They also begin to master themselves and their environment. To make the most of these new capabilities, teenagers must give up some of the childhood ideas and dependencies that have provided a great deal of security. Younger children are not self-conscious about their bodies. They can be comfortably dependent on their parents. Younger children have clear ideas about right and wrong and can avoid feeling guilty by behaving the way their parents want

61

them to. They have goals that can usually be reached, they are not frequently disappointed for long. Giving up these childhood securities means becoming vulnerable and perhaps losing self-esteem. Although it is not usual, if the loss of self-esteem lasts for more than a couple of weeks, it may lead to a serious depression.

CHAPTER 5

Giving In and Giving Up—
Suicide

"I'll see you tomorrow," promised Cindy as she left the guidance counselor's office. "I'll bring the pictures." Cindy and the counselor met for about forty-five minutes at least once a week. Several months earlier, a health education teacher had noticed that Cindy's interest and enthusiasm for volleyball was waning. At the beginning of the term, Cindy had been so skillful that her teammates urged her to audition for the state league. Then the teacher noticed that Cindy seemed preoccupied, sad, and moody. She had lost five pounds and appeared listless.

Over the past two months Cindy had revealed her feelings of loneliness to her counselor. Cindy didn't make friends easily. In fact, she had only three friends. She worried that these few would find her dull and unattractive and desert her. One of the three was Ricky, a senior and star forward on the school's basketball team. His friendship meant everything to Cindy, and she frequently fantasized about their future together. Recently she had heard rumors that Ricky was interested in another girl, but Cindy was reluctant to believe gossip. She told the counselor about her fear of rejection and said she didn't think she could handle it. Cindy couldn't chance a confrontation with Ricky, although she felt the relationship was changing. Without Ricky, Cindy believed there was no future for her. The counselor continued to reassure Cindy that her attractiveness and warm personality would interest many more young men.

Today Cindy's conversation was full of Ricky and their plans. He had accompanied her on a family picnic. He had asked her to go to a movie with him and had planned a day at the beach. Sixteen and in love, Cindy was exuberant again. She had expressed a renewed interest in volleyball and said she planned to return to the team. Cindy smiled happily as she waved good-bye to the counselor. When Cindy arrived home, she found a note from Ricky. He told her about his new love. The loss of Ricky meant failure, rejection, and loss of self-esteem to Cindy, leading to excruciating pain and stress followed by depression. One hour after she left school, Cindy jumped to her death from the roof of the sixteen-story apartment house where she lived.

Depression is one of the leading causes of suicide in adolescents and adults. Dr. Michael Peck, consultant to the Suicide Prevention Center in Los Angeles, California, says that there are different types of adolescent suicide; one he calls crisis suicide. This is like Cindy's situation, where sudden traumatic changes occur in an adolescent's life, leading to unbearable stress and a desire to end it all.

Youths who act out depression fall into another category. The number of adolescents in this group is on the increase. These teenagers behave in ways seen by others as illegal, harmful, and dangerous. They may engage in alcohol and drug abuse; they may run away, shoplift, or commit serious violence. These young people may feel depressed during their early youth and may mistake their depression for boredom. Then they may use alcohol and drugs to dispel these bad feelings.

Before 1965, suicide rates in the United States and in much of the world increased directly with age. Thus, the fewest suicides occurred among the young; moderate suicide rates were found among those in their middle years; and the highest number of suicides occurred among old people. In the late 1960s, the suicide rate among young people began increasing. This increase has continued until the present.

How can we tell when a young person is likely to commit suicide? There aren't too many studies on young people, but experts do know that it's not just an impulsive act. There is usually a history of psychiatric disorder including depression, or the young person may have suffered an unusual amount of stress. The cause of most teenage suicide seems to be a deep, personal sense of loss.

Reasons for the Increase in Teenage Suicide

Those who have studied this subject offer several reasons for the increase in teenage suicide. All agree that probably never before have adolescents been exposed to such a variety of tensions and social changes. And never have youth been so ill-equipped to meet them.

Peck and Litman, in "Current Trends in Youthful Suicide," cite the relationship of the population explosion of the late 1940s and early 1950s to the youth suicide phenomenon. "Children born between 1950 and 1955 passed through their teens and early twenties during the period the suicide rate was rising most rapidly. The population in this age group was higher than it had ever been before and was certainly out of proportion to other age groups in size. It is possible that an overcrowding phenomenon occurred in this generation that resulted in too many young people wanting too many things that were not available, contributing to an increased feeling of anonymity and alienation." Again a loss of self-esteem and personal value, and a sense of defeat.

Medical experts believe one out of ten adolescents is "at risk." This means that they have not only thought about killing themselves but have planned it. But no one knows the full extent of the problem, because so many suicides are not reported as such in order to spare loved ones the pain and stigma of suicide.

Dr. Everett Dulit, director of Child and Adolescent Psychiatry at Montefiore Hospital in the Bronx, New York, says that experience leads him to believe that those who commit suicide tend to be suffering from some type of depression. "Such youngsters represent about two-thirds of all adolescent suicides," he says.

In October 1984, the Senate Judiciary Subcommittee on Juvenile Justice, which is concerned with the rise in the adolescent suicide rate, heard testimony from a youngster who had made three attempts to end her life. The sixteen-year-old, from Washington, D.C., spoke of her depression. She said she disliked herself, and she admitted that the pain of kidney and back problems contributed to her suicide attempts. She began isolating herself from other people, she said, which deepened her depression. She cut her wrists on impulse when she was thirteen, later tried to starve herself, and then took an overdose of pills and cut her wrists again. Her mother reported that her daughter was angry at everything and everyone.

When Is It for Real?

How do you decide if an adolescent is mildly depressed, severely depressed, or suicidal? Dr. Joseph Warshaw, consultant to the Young Adult Clinic in Dallas, Texas, believes it's helpful to use specific criteria in diagnosing depression. A depression, he says, "includes other things beside being unhappy. It includes a time factor—a period of unhappiness that should continue for at least a couple of weeks. There should also be changes in certain body functions, for instance, sleep and appetite changes or disturbances, lack of concentration and involvement. One should also look for a tendency in the youth to blame himself for everything. And finally there is suicide ideation [thinking about suicide]. These symptoms [mark] the depression syndrome that is more than 'being unhappy' and precedes suicide."

Many adolescents think and talk about suicide. Even their poetry and diaries reflect this interest. They frequently proclaim that they feel worthless and that everyone would be better off without them. They say they would welcome death. "I don't want to live" or "I want to go to sleep and never wake up" are pleas that need attention.

CHAPTER 6

What Makes It Go Away

The worst thing about a depression is how terrible it feels. When you are with someone who is severely depressed, you can actually feel that person's pain. A depression can also affect every aspect of a teenager's life, from the ability to concentrate on a homework assignment to the capacity to make friends. The past, present, and future can look like one long series of failures. The only good thing about a depression is that you *can* recover from it. Just knowing and accepting this fact is frequently the first and most important step toward recovery.

Obstacles to Treatment

Because hopelessness is a common symptom of depression, the depressed teenager often feels that things will not get better in the future. Believing this, he or she might not seek help. Some parents and teachers also fail to see a teenager's unhappiness as a treatable condition. They believe that sadness is a normal part of the turbulent adolescent years, or they see isolation and the lack of enthusiasm as part of the teenager's personality. Doctors frequently see depressed teenagers and miss making the diagnosis. They may pay attention to their patients' headaches and tell them to take a couple of aspirin. They may notice the chronic tiredness and advise the teenagers to go to bed earlier or to eat a more balanced diet. Too often, they do not put all of the pieces together, and they miss the fact that their patients have a serious but treatable disease.

The fact that many adults overlook teenage depression has been strikingly documented by an adolescent mental health center in New York City. The center's therapists talked to guidance counselors and principals of nearby junior and senior high schools, asking them to look for students who were withdrawn, unhappy, and functioning below their academic potential. Most of the teenagers who were referred for evaluations had chronic and serious depressions.

The Importance of Treatment

This is all very discouraging for a number of reasons. First, as noted in Chapter 1, many teenagers do have depressions and continue to feel intensely unhappy for much longer than is necessary. Second, depressed teenagers' ability to function in almost every aspect of life is compromised. The young person should be learning and accomplishing, but this doesn't happen when a person is suffering from a depression. As a result, these years are lost. Others are moving ahead, but depressed teenagers are left behind with many things undone. Third, aside from learning specific skills, teenagers are also establishing a self-image, which they will take into adulthood. If this image is positive, the teenagers will approach adulthood with enthusiasm and confidence, and this attitude can lead to success and fulfillment. It is hard for depressed adolescents to succeed, however. With effort, they may have some successes and some good moments, but they tend to forget these positive times and see everything in negative terms. Because of this, it is almost certain that low self-esteem will continue beyond the teenage years for someone who has a long-term depression. This is a burden for young adults, even after they are no longer depressed. They expect failure in everything from business to love. This prevents them from even trying. Beth, at nineteen, faced this situation.

The most frequent answer Beth gave to friends, employers, and others was, "What for?" At one time, she was one of the happy-go-lucky kids in junior college. But after she failed to get the lead in a play, she seemed to withdraw from everybody and everything. She ran for class secretary halfheartedly, but didn't get elected. Beth also failed to make the debating team. Beth's counselor suggested that she try for the Robert Louis Stevenson Prize in Short Stories. Beth replied, "What for? I won't get it. I'm a loser." The counselor reminded her of her A average in English and her published stories. But Beth was unconvinced. She continued to lose faith in herself.

There is a clear-cut connection between teenage

depression and suicide. There is every reason to believe that effective early treatment of depressed young people can prevent many suicides.

What to Look For

If parents, teachers, doctors, friends, or the young people themselves notice any of the following symptoms, they should consider the possibility that a depression is occurring:

1. Moods that jump around from boredom and indifference to high-pressured talking and activity. These teenagers may laugh at times, but their laughter is empty. Even when they fool around, they don't really look as if they are having fun. Thrill seeking, such as fast and reckless driving or drug use, may provide a temporary escape from unhappiness.
2. Chronic tiredness and lack of energy. Illnesses such as anemia or thyroid disease can also cause these symptoms, but these conditions can be quickly diagnosed by a physician.
3. Chronic nausea, chest pain, back pain, stomach pain, constipation, muscle aches, headaches, loss of appetite. Again, a physician can check out these symptoms to see if they have a physical basis.
4. Having difficulty falling asleep, awakening during the night and not falling back to sleep quickly, or waking up too early in the morning.

5. Hypersensitivity, with an overreaction to criticism, and the inability to satisfy self. These young people feel uneasy when things work out well, as though they do not deserve success and are waiting for the bad news. Sometimes, when on the verge of success, they ruin things for themselves.

6. Irritability, with outbursts of anger over minor things. This may lead to sarcasm or to hostility toward authorities such as parents and teachers. There may be physical fights with friends as well as enemies. At home, this may lead to running away. Some of this provocative behavior may be an attempt to elicit punishment.

7. The constant seeking of love and approval. Teenagers will look with desperation to family members, teachers, and peers for reassurance that they are worthy. No matter how much praise or attention they get, it is still not enough. Increased sexual activity may be a part of this picture, as teenagers look for closeness and reassurance; they may be repeatedly disappointed in their relationships.

8. A decline in academic performance. With the inability to concentrate and chronic tiredness, it is very difficult for most depressed teenagers to perform close to their real ability.

9. Constant self-criticism. Teenagers may put themselves down, presenting themselves and their activities as inferior. They feel a sweeping sense of being "stupid" or "evil." They may also think that everyone would be better off if they

were dead. This can lead to specific thoughts of suicide.

The Initial Assessment

If the suspicion of depression exists, a physician with a lot of experience in treating adolescents is probably in the best position to make an initial assessment. The doctor should understand normal adolescent psychosocial development and be able to evaluate any physical conditions that might produce symptoms of depression. A physician who has known the young person for a number of years has the additional advantage of being able to compare current and past behavior.

A variety of mental health professionals, such as psychiatrists, psychologists, and psychiatric social workers, can make this same assessment with the assistance of a physician who can rule out the presence of physical illness. The professional will usually talk to the parents so as to get a better picture of what is going on at home as well as at school. He or she will also want to compare the situation with earlier times. Some teenagers don't like this idea, especially if they have not been getting along with their parents. They fear that their parents are just going to criticize them for failing grades, misbehavior, or bad tempers. Parents may very well be angry with their teenager at this point, so that the teenager has some realistic concern about what the parents will say. A good professional should be able to get the necessary information without hurting anyone's feelings. Sometimes concerned parents appear angry to their depressed son or daughter. In the presence of the professional, however, the parents may be able to express their true concern to their teenager without anger and resentment. Some parents may see their child as lazy, insolent, or bad, not realizing that a depression is at the bottom of the adolescent's behavior. Parental anger and criticism will just make things worse for a son or daughter who already feels bad.

This happened with Kenneth and his mother. His grades had dropped sharply, and he was skipping school for the first time. This upset his mother, who had always taken pride in her son's academic excellence. What was most difficult for her was Kenneth's behavior toward his two-year-old niece, who lived with them. He had appeared to love her, had taken care of her, and had enjoyed playing with her until a couple of months ago. But shortly after his grades began to drop, he started to become angry with his niece while they were playing. Once when she did not do what he wanted her to, Kenneth became enraged and struck her hard. His mother was horrified and began to think of her son as a bad and thankless child. The school guidance counselor referred Kenneth to a psychiatrist, who diagnosed him as having a major depression. The psychiatrist explained to Kenneth's mother that her son was still the same good child whom she had always known. Kenneth did love his niece and was just as upset by his own behavior as his mother was. Once his mother understood that Kenneth's mental disorder was a depression and not a moral problem, she was able to be much more understanding and supportive. Her attitude toward Kenneth no longer reinforced his own view of himself as a terrible person.

The realization that a teenager is suffering from a

specific disorder that can be treated is usually a great relief to everyone, including the teenager. One depressed sixteen-year-old girl was irritable, withdrawn, and a truant. Her mother understood the situation very well, however. She said, "You are not lazy or bad. Something is wrong, and you need to see a doctor for treatment."

Treatment for Reactive Depression

Once the problem is identified, specific treatment is determined that will reduce the depression and the circumstances that are contributing to it. John's family had moved in the middle of the school year from an apartment in Manhattan to a large and beautiful home on Staten Island. Although he was not really far away, John was able to see his old friends only on weekends. At his new school, groups of friends had already been formed, and it was hard for him to fit in. He decided to put his energy into his studies during the week so that he would have more time to visit Manhattan on weekends. He found himself behind in several of his classes because his new teachers seemed to expect more of students, and they covered more material than John was used to learning.

When midterm grades were posted, John found that he had done quite poorly. His parents decided that John should spend most of his weekends studying. Although John stayed home, he spent most of his time feeling resentful toward his parents for grounding him. He was also angry that they had moved in the first place. He was not able to concentrate on his studies and fell further and further behind. He would worry about his grades at night and not be able to fall asleep. In school John had trouble paying attention and became angry with his teachers for going too fast. At first, John's teachers were understanding, but as he became angry and sarcastic with them, they lost patience. He also began to pick fights with some of the students who had initially rejected him.

At this point a guidance counselor was called in. John's behavior toward teachers and the other students was becoming a problem in the classroom. The guidance counselor saw how unhappy John was behind this angry front. He wanted to do well and be respected by the teachers and students, but more and more, he felt that the situation was hopeless. Once the counselor knew the whole story, she began to try to make things better for him. The teachers were told of John's desire to do well and of his real need for help with his schoolwork. John met with a tutor a couple of times a week after school. The counselor convinced his parents to let John spend one day each weekend with his old friends, if he would study the other day. The guidance counselor followed John's progress and encouraged him. It was a lot of hard work, but John's ability to concentrate returned, and his anger toward his teachers decreased. Once he saw that things were improving, his cheerfulness returned, and he began to make friends in his new school.

What was it that the counselor did that could account for this dramatic change? Maybe she didn't do anything, and everything would have worked out fine anyway. This seems unlikely, though, because when things start to go wrong, the disasters have a way of reinforcing negative attitudes and behavior, and this just makes things worse. The counselor's intervention with both parents and teachers stopped them from making John feel even worse about himself than he already did. The available source of positive feelings, his old friends, was returned, but the importance of studying and catching up was not ignored. His tutoring and one weekend day of hard studying allowed him to improve his grades. By listening to him and showing that she understood his position, the counselor also demonstrated her respect and concern for him. His resentment over the situation was understandable, and to some extent justified. She acknowledged this. With her help, he was able to regain a sense of control over his life.

Treatment for Depression Resulting from Physical Illness

The loss of good health frequently leads to the inability to participate in sports, attend school, and do things with friends. Even in emotionally healthy people, this kind of loss can cause a reactive depression. Sharon was fifteen years old and was about three-quarters of the way through a year's treatment of chemotherapy for osteosarcoma (cancer of the bone). The disease appeared to be cured, but she was unable to think of herself as having a future or as being better. She had lost all of her hair temporarily as a result of the chemotherapy. Some bone had been surgically removed from her leg at the site of the tumor, and she needed physical rehabilitation to regain her ability to walk well. She experienced extreme nausea and vomiting after each chemotherapy treatment. Sharon complained of insomnia and chest pains, and she feared that her heart had been damaged. She said that she was too tired and weak to do her exercises. She was irritable and confused. Sharon was unable to do any of the schoolwork her home tutor assigned her. She was tearful and angry and would say repeatedly, "Something has been taken away from me." Some of her physical symptoms were a direct result of her chemotherapy, but the hopelessness and the inability to do anything were the result of a depression.

Sharon's doctor intervened to move her out of this hopeless position. He let her control the timing of her treatments, and discussed everything with her before performing any tests or medical procedures. He encouraged her to participate in rehabilitation so that she could begin to overcome her fear of physical disability. He also gave her an opportunity to talk about her fears and frustrations. In two or three weeks, her depressed mood began to lift. Her activity level increased dramatically, as she began to exercise hard in order to master the ability to walk without a limp. Sharon began to study and to speak with some enthusiasm about returning to school. Even the nausea and vomiting decreased.

The illness and its treatment made Sharon feel passive and helpless. This produced a depression, which made it even more difficult for her to do things for herself when she was physically able. She began to improve after she got more control over her life and took the necessary steps to regain her feeling of mastery. As with John, the capability was there but was being blocked by a depression and by unresponsive people. With encouragement, both John and Sharon were able to make use of their own strengths, once others began to work with them, instead of against them. In a somewhat similar situation, Kevin's illness was complicated by a family problem.

Kevin's father left the family when Kevin was a small child. His mother worked at two jobs to support the three children. At the age of nine, Kevin was hit by a truck while riding his bicycle. He was seriously injured and later had to undergo surgery for the removal of a kidney. For the next few years, he functioned well. But at sixteen, Kevin had to limit all physical exercise, follow a strict diet, and take medication daily. These measures made it impossible for him to attend school. Finally, it became evident that he would need a kidney transplant. He was bedridden, depressed, and hostile toward everyone. He began to feel sorry for himself and thought of dying. The doctors tried to find his father, who would be an excellent kidney donor. They spent precious weeks trying to locate him while Kevin's condition grew worse. He blamed his mother for not having kept in touch with his father. Finally Kevin had to be hospitalized. His mother was found to be compatible, and she gave Kevin one of her kidneys. Kevin's physical condition improved slowly, and he was able to leave the hospital within three weeks.

At home, Kevin brooded about the father he never knew. His brothers and sisters also began to show an interest in learning about him. Kevin put all of his energies into searching through old papers, questioning family friends and relatives. He became so involved in this project that he didn't eat or take his medication. The social worker learned of the true state of affairs when Kevin did not keep his follow-up appointments.

She visited the home and talked with Kevin. She offered to help him contact an agency that specialized in finding relatives. Once the procedures had started, Kevin began to come out of his depression. He felt good and no longer blamed anyone for his mishap. He took pictures of everyone to help the agency in its search; the whole family became closer and looked forward to the possibility of having a complete family someday.

Treatment of Chronic Mild Depression

After a teenager has been depressed for a long time, complete recovery becomes more difficult. This kind of situation was described in Chapter 1 in the story of Sandra, who was not able to remember a time of feeling good.

Given this situation, the simple interventions described for a reactive depression are usually inadequate. First, a therapist's interest and understanding will not increase the teenager's self-respect. Sandra's needs are too great, and the therapist will just be one more person who fails to meet them. Second, it will be hard to get Sandra to try things at which she has already failed. Third, even if Sandra does begin to feel a little better and to change, it will be hard for her to become a part of the family after being excluded as the irresponsible, thankless child for such a long time.

Such a situation may require a combination of individual and family treatment before any real improvement occurs. Each therapist has his or her own individual style and will approach Sandra and her family a little differently, but a few basic techniques are required. For Sandra to improve significantly, the family has to be ready and willing to let her change. There will be some resistance to this, because it will disrupt family life. Even though everyone will be better off in the long run, change produces anxiety. Sandra's mother and sister must give up the comfort of their special relationship with each other to let Sandra in. If they are unable to do this, they may make it very difficult for Sandra to become a loving, responsible, and happy child because her changes will be discouraged. More than one or two family meetings are required to bring about change in this well-established family system. Regular family therapy sessions with a trained and experienced family therapist are frequently necessary.

Sandra must see herself in a different light before she can begin to behave differently. Some therapists would try to help Sandra understand her current behavior and feelings in the light of her previous losses and disappointments. The intention is to have her see that she is not responsible for her father's leaving. Many times children believe that there is something wrong with them which caused a parent to leave and reject them. With time, if Sandra can rid herself of the idea that something is wrong or bad about her, she may be able to change her attitude and take some risks. She may be able to reach out to her family and to new friends. Slowly, she can rebuild her confidence through small successes with the support of her therapist. Bringing about such changes will require hard work and months of therapy, but the alternative for Sandra is probably an adulthood of continuing disappointments.

Group therapy could provide additional help for someone like Sandra. Once she begins to see that she is not such a bad person, the group may provide some support. She may also find that a lot of her fears and her lack of confidence are shared by other teenagers. Sandra will see that she is not really so different from others. If she does approach friends in a way that turns them off, group members might point this out to her in a constructive way. She may have learned this ineffective behavior before, when she still felt that no one really wanted her as a friend. Once Sandra feels better about herself, she will be able to unlearn this behavior, if she is made aware of it.

With a long-term depression and its associated low self-image, the more sources of support, the better the chances for change and long-term success.

Treatment of a Major Depression

Even with a supportive counselor, doctor, or therapist and a responsive environment, some young people remain depressed. It seems that no matter how hard they try and no matter how hard their families and friends try to help, they just don't feel any better. For many of these teenagers, talking about their problems with a therapist is difficult and painful, and may even make them feel worse. In some cases, therapy is terminated with no change or even a worsening of the depression. The depressed teenagers and their families then feel even more frustrated and discouraged. In this kind of depression, biological changes have probably taken place in the teenager's nervous system, creating another obstacle to improvement. In addition to being more severe, this kind of depression seems to actually have a significant physical quality. The victim may have no energy and may be tired constantly. To the observer, depressed teenagers may look as though they are carrying a weight around on their shoulders, or as if they have a ball and chain fastened to their ankles. They frequently have difficulty sleeping and concentrating. One girl described her thinking as "fuzzy," as she struggled unsuccessfully to keep up with her classes at school.

Antidepressant Medication

With a major depression, if therapy and environmental intervention do not begin to help in about a month, then medication should be considered. Because all drugs have possible side effects, no medication should ever be taken for anything unless there are clear-cut reasons for its use and a physician recommends it. The medications used for depression are called antidepressants; they came into use in the late 1950s. They are not physically addictive and do not produce a "high." They are not direct simulants like amphetamines (speed) or Ritalin. For this reason, they are not abused, and the patient has no difficulty in eliminating them.

Because they re-establish a balance of naturally occurring chemicals in the brain, it can take one to six weeks before they begin to help a depressed person feel better. During the first couple of weeks, side effects, such as a dry mouth and light-headedness, may occur, so that the affected teenager may actually feel worse for a while. This can lead to discouragement and the refusal to take the medication. Unfortunately, the most common cause of medication failure appears to be giving up and stopping it too soon.

Another drug that has recently received a lot of attention is a chemical element called lithium. In 1949, an Australian psychiatrist, John Cade, discovered its effectiveness in treating mania. It is not a treatment for depression, but may prevent a depression from occurring if taken beforehand. This is used most commonly for people with manic-depressive disorders. At first, there was a lot of concern about heart and kidney damage from lithium. Further study has shown, however, that there is little danger if the drug is prescribed carefully, using blood tests to determine dosage.

Other newer antidepressants are now being tried. None of them are clearly superior to the older ones, but considering the tremendous medical advances in the last thirty years, there is every reason to believe that more effective and specific drugs will someday be discovered for the treatment of the different kinds of depression.

Electroconvulsive Therapy

With the introduction of the different antidepressant drugs, electroconvulsive therapy (ECT, also called shock therapy) is used less frequently. This procedure was first reported in 1939 by two Italian psychiatrists, Cerlette and Bini. They caused convulsions in patients by passing electric current through the brain by means of two electrodes placed on the forehead. It is a very effective treatment of severe depression. Since that time, both a short-acting anesthetic and muscle-paralyzing agent have been added to the ECT to make it less frightening and to prevent injury during the convulsion. There has always been concern about the possibility of permanent brain damage from this treatment. None of the many studies done to test this has demonstrated brain damage or a permanent decrease in cognitive capacity. Some clinicians induce the seizure only over the nondominant hemisphere (usually the right side of the brain) to decrease the amount of temporary confusion and memory loss that follows immediately after the convulsion.

Many people have strong feelings about the use of ECT, possibly because it seems so dangerous and hurtful. Others think it is used to punish bad patients. It is quite possible that has happened. Regardless of these concerns, ECT is safe when administered carefully and continues to be used for people with severe depressions who do not respond to antidepressants. Considering the disabling nature of a severe long-term depression and the risk of suicide, the use of ECT has its place even for adolescents with severe depression that does not improve with other treatments.

Psychotherapy for Major Depression

Once a depression has been successfully treated by antidepressants or ECT, there is still work to be done. If the depression was severe and long, many pieces of the teen's life will have to be put back in order. Some friends may have been lost. Schoolwork and grades may have suffered. Family relations may also be strained. An understanding counselor can help the recovering teenager organize and approach this work. Some environmental intervention on behalf of the teenager may also be needed so that teachers and family will give him or her time to recover before having to face the regular demands.

In addition, after having gone through such an experience, teenagers' images of themselves may have changed for the worse. Because these are the years when a person's self-image is developing, self-confidence may be eroded by a depression, even after recovery. It is important for the teenager to have the opportunity to put this experience in its place by better understanding what he or she went through. Psychotherapy can help a teenager regain self-confidence, but only after the depression has begun to improve.

One more thing can be dealt with in psychotherapy. After the occurrence of a depression in a teenager, we know that an increased possibility of future depressions exists. One way to prevent a second depression is to continue using antidepressants for six to nine months at a reduced dosage. This takes care of the biological part of depression for that period, but we know that there is often a significant psychological part also. If this teenager is particularly vulnerable to psychological stress or loss, perhaps because of early childhood disruptions, psychotherapy may be able to change that. For example, people who are very dependent appear to be vulnerable to loss. Psychotherapy may reduce this dependency. These changes do not come quickly or easily. Many teenagers will not have the motivation,

once they feel better, to make psychotherapy worthwhile. It is a very individual thing; some people can
make better use of this kind of psychotherapy as older
adolescents or young adults. It is good for an interested
teenager to have the chance at any age.

The Therapists

Depressed teenagers can get treatment from various
mental health professionals. They should also keep in
mind that clergy and guidance counselors can be helpful when a little supportive counseling is needed. Those
who need an antidepressant must remember that only a
doctor can prescribe medication; these teenagers should
see a psychiatrist or their family physician. It is important to choose a therapist who is experienced in working with teenagers and who likes this age group. It is also
important for both the adolescent and his or her family
to have confidence in and respect for the therapist. After
the first couple of meetings, a decision should be made
whether this is the right therapist. If the relationship
between the teenager and therapist does not feel right
at that time, then the teenager should try again with
someone else. Once he or she has chosen a suitable
therapist, it is best to stay with the same one through the
good and bad times. Only then can real change occur.
It is worth the effort.

BIBLIOGRAPHY

Abraham K. *Notes on the Psychoanalytical Investigation and Treatment of Manic-depressive Insanity and Allied Conditions. Selected Papers on Psychoanalysis.* London: Hogarth Press, 1927.

Arieti, S., and Chzanowski, G. (eds.). *New Dimensions in Psychiatry: A World Review.* New York: John Wiley & Sons, 1976.

Cherlin, A. J. *Marriage, Divorce, Remarriage.* Cambridge: Harvard University Press, 1978.

Chiles, J. A., Miller, M. L., and Cox, G. E. "Depression in an Adolescent Delinquent Population." *Arch. Gen Psychiatry* 37:1179–84, 1980.

Freud S. *Mourning and Melancholia.* Standard Edition, Complete Works. London, Vol. XIV, 1957.

Hudgens, R. W. *Psychiatric Disorders in Adolescents.* Baltimore: Williams & Wilkins, 1974.

Hudgens, R. W., Morrison, J. R., and Barchha, R. G. "Life events and Onset of Primary Affective Disorders." *Arch. Gen. Psychiatry* 16:134–45, 1967.

Inamdar, S. C., Siomopoulos, G., Osborn, M., and Bianchi, E. "Phenomenology Associated with Depressed Moods in Adolescents." *Am. J. Psychiatry,* 136:2, 156–59, February, 1979.

Jacobsen, S., Fasman, J., and Dimascio, A. "Deprivation in the Childhood of Depressed Women." *J. Nerv. Ment. Dis.* 161:5, 1975.

Kandel, D. E., and Davies, M. "Epidemiology of Depressive Mood in Adolescents." *Arch. Gen. Psychiatry.* 1982:39, 1205–12.

Lahmeyer, H. W., Poznanski, E. O., and Bellur Srinath, N. "EEG Sleep in Depressed Adolescents," *Am. J. Psychiatry* 140:9, September 1983, 1150–53.

Lindemann, E. "Symptomatology and Management of Acute Grief." *Am. J. Psychiatry.* 101:141, 1944.

Offer, D., Ostrov, E., and Howard, K. "The Mental Health Professionals' Concept of the Normal Adolescent." *Arch. Gen. Psychiatry.* 38: February 1981, 149–52.

Peck, M. L. "Categories of Adolescent Suicide Differentiated." *Roche Report: Frontiers of Psychiatry,* World-Wide Medical Press, 1980.

Peck, M. L., and Litman, R. "Current Trends in Youthful Suicide." In J. Burke (ed.), *Suicides and Blacks,* Fannor Research and Developmental Center, 1975 pp. 13–27.

Rutter, M., Graham, P., Chadwick, O., and Yule, W. "Adolescent Turmoil: Fact or Fiction." *J. Child Psychol. Psychiat.,* 17:35–36, 1976.

Strober, M. "Clinical and Biological Perspectives on Depressive Disorders in Adolescence." In Cantwell and G. Carlson (eds.), *Affective Disorders in Childhood and Adolescence.* New York: Spectrum, 1984.

Wallenstein, J. D., and Kelly, J. B. *Surviving the Breakup: How Children and Parents Cope with Divorce.* New York: Basic Books, 1980.

Weiss, R. S. *Going It Alone: The Family Life and Social Situation of the Single Parent.* New York: Basic Books, 1979.

Weissman, M. M., Leckman, J.F., Merikangas, K. R., Gammon, D. G., and Prusoff, B. A. "Depression and Anxiety Disorders in Parents and Children." *Arch. Gen. Psychiatry,* 17, September 1984, 845–52.

SUGGESTED FURTHER READINGS

Benson, Herbert. *Relaxation Responses.* New York: Avon, 1978.

Brooks, Bruce. *The Moves Make the Man.* New York: Harper & Row, 1984.

Cohen, Susan, and Daniel Cohen. *Teenage Stress.* New York: Evans, 1984.

Eagan, Andrea. *Why Am I So Miserable If These Are The Best Years of My Life?* Philadelphia: Lippincott, 1976.

Harris, Thomas. *Staying O. K.* New York: Harper & Row, 1985.

Laiken, Diedre, and Allen Schneider. *Listen To Me, I'm Angry.* New York: Lothrop, 1980.

Rosenberg, Ellen. *Growing Up Feeling Good.* New York: Beaufort Books, 1983.

Zindel, Paul. *Harry and Hortense at Hormone High.* New York: Harper & Row, 1984.

INDEX

DOWN IS NOT OUT

94

ABOUT THE AUTHORS

ESSIE E. LEE, a professor of Community Health Education at Hunter College, New York, has a background in health, guidance, and education. Dr. Lee, a graduate of Columbia University, has devoted many years to research, prevention, and intervention techniques and strategies in the field of drug addiction. A former nurse, counselor, and teacher, she finds that these occupations have helped to formulate concepts for the practice of preventive medicine, another one of her interests. Dr. Lee serves on several boards, foundations, and health service organizations. Her leisure activities include sports fishing, travel, and collecting Asian artifacts. Dr. Lee writes about a variety of topics including health careers, alcohol, women, marriage and families, and the use of computers in the health sciences.

RICHARD WORTMAN was born and raised in Pittsburgh, Pennsylvania. He received a B.A. in English literature from Kenyon College and graduated from Northwestern University Medical School. His specialty training was in adolescent psychiatry at Mount Sinai Medical Center in New York City.

Dr. Wortman works with young adults at the Adolescent Health Center of Mount Sinai. He has run seminars and workshops for young people and teachers in such areas as depression and suicide, drug and alcohol use, and adolescent development. Dr. Wortman resides in Manhattan with his wife and three children.

06905.

616.85
LEE
Lee, Essie E.

8.99

616.85
LEE
Lee, Essie E.
Down is not out

06905

DATE DUE	BORROWER'S NAME	
9/17	V. Skinner	1
NO1 6'94	Totman	147
EE1 '95	Ann Reeves	126
12/23/98	Kyle Benson DUSSOURD	Donah